About the Author

Jon Sandifer has over 20 years' experience in Eastern healing traditions including feng shui, Nine Star Ki, oriental diagnosis and acupressure. He is one of the leading exponents of feng shui in the UK and is currently Chairperson of the Feng Shui Society. Jon lectures on feng shui and feng shui astrology throughout the United Kingdom and the United States and is the author of several books including *Feng Shui Astrology*, *Acupressure* and *The 10 Day Rebalance Programme*.

For my wife Renata

Feng Shui

PIATKUS

Piatkus Guides

Other titles in this series include:

Celtic Wisdom
Crystal Wisdom
The Essential Nostradamus
Meditation
Tarot

A PIATKUS GUIDE

Feng Shui

Jon Sandifer

PIATKUS

First published in 1999 by
Judy Piatkus (Publishers) Ltd
5 Windmill Street, London W1P 1HF

ISBN 0-7499-1870-5

Set in 12.5/14pt Perpetua
Typeset by Action Publishing Technology Ltd, Gloucester
Printed & bound in Great Britain by
Mackays of Chatham PLC

Contents

Acknowledgements

To Judy Piatkus for her encouragement and support. To my editors Anne Lawrence, Jill Foulston and Gill Cormode for their insights and enthusiasm for the project.

Many thanks to my colleagues Stephen Skinner, Sue Reynolds, Richard Creightmore and Cathryn McNaughton for taking the time to read the manuscript and giving me their feedback.

To my friends in the feng shui world who are doing so much to make this fascinating subject available to so many: Denise Linn, Karen Kingston, Roger Green, Tony Holdsworth, William Spear, Gina Lazenby, Jan Cisek, and James Moser.

To the current and past committee members of the Feng Shui Society who give their time to promote feng shui.

For Leslie and June for lending me their wonderful boathouse on the Thames to write the book.

Thank you all.

Introduction

During the past 30 years, thousands of Westerners have enjoyed the benefits of using a variety of different healing systems and nutritional programmes that originate in the East, whether this has involved a consultation with an acupuncturist, or an evening course in tai chi, yoga or chi kung, or perhaps having had shiatsu treatment. If you asked for tofu in your local supermarket 30 years ago, you would have been greeted with a blank expression from the sales assistant. Nowadays, there is a far greater awareness of Oriental healing and dietary systems and more and more people are familiar with terms such as yin and yang, chi, feng shui or chi kung.

The past decade has seen the growth of a tremendous interest in feng shui in the West. Over 300 books are currently available on the subject, weekend seminars have been designed to introduce the basics, in-depth courses offer training to professionals and a glossy magazine is now available worldwide. National newspapers, magazines, radio programmes and television shows, have carried reports and articles on the subject. In 1997 the *Daily Mail* began a regular column featuring questions and answers on topics related to feng shui, Wimpey Homes produced a booklet for prospective homebuyers entitled *Feng Shui in Your Home* and Queens Park Rangers Football Club employed a feng shui consultant to give them advice.

Naturally, businesses with a connection in the Far East are reported to consult feng shui experts – the Hyatt Regency Hotel in Singapore, the Hong Kong Shanghai Bank in Hong Kong and the Marks & Spencer branch in Hong Kong have all sought feng shui advice. Hong Kong-based Hutchinson Communication – Orange – has used the principles in opening new networks for their mobile telephone network.

The Contents of this Book

Feng shui is a rich and diverse subject with many different schools of thought and styles. In Chapter 2 I outline the history of feng shui and describe the development of the different schools.

Integral to all the schools of feng shui are the underlying principles. In Chapter 3 I take you through these step by step, making them practical for your future study and practice of feng shui. Getting to grips with the concept of chi, looking at the working dynamics of yin and yang, understanding the relationship of the Five Elements – all help to give this fascinating subject more depth as you explore it for yourself.

Chapters 4, 5 and 6 show you how to apply the theory to your own home. I will show you how you can analyse a room, your entire home or plot by placing the pa kua over the floor plan of your home. By determining the nature that each sector of your home represents, you can begin to bring in appropriate changes – in line with what you would like to achieve.

In Chapter 7 I outline other systems and fields of study that can create more harmony for you and your environment. These include: space clearing, Nine Star Ki Astrology, geopathic stress and electromagnetic stress.

Finally, I leave you with an excellent resource list to enable you to take the subject further. This includes a reading list, details of courses and addresses of practitioners and places where you can buy many of the feng shui tools that I recommend.

Feng shui is an enormous subject. In this book you can begin to take on the essence of the subject and, with time and practice, begin to peel back the layers and discover more of its richness. There is much more to find out, particularly if you choose to take on the astrological dimension of feng shui. Begin with the basics and these will provide a fine foundation for you to take the subject further.

About the Author

My own background with feng shui began when I studied the principles of yin and yang, initially by reading the *Tao Te Ching* in 1972 and later studying the *I Ching*. In 1977 I took my interest further by studying and later teaching one of the astrologies of the *I Ching* – Nine House Astrology. During my research into the subject I began to take a deeper interest in 'Directionology' and this opened up a new avenue which led me to feng shui.

I spent many years practising and teaching shiatsu massage, macrobiotics and Oriental diagnosis. Initially, I felt that feng shui provided a useful additional insight into Oriental diagnosis. Everything about our health, our happiness, our destiny can potentially be revealed in our habits, lifestyle, expression, symptoms and living space. In my opinion, it was just as important to take into consideration *where* a person was living alongside *how* they were living, as defined by their diet, lifestyle and levels of physical activity. It became apparent to me that there was no division in these areas of our lives in terms of our health and well-being.

In 1994 I offered to help the Feng Shui Society by offering my experience and insights regarding setting standards and a code of ethics for feng shui practitioners and students. During the 1980s I had done similar work for both the Shiatsu Society and the Macrobiotic Association. Currently I am Chairman of the Feng Shui Society, I practise as a feng shui consultant and I teach feng shui and feng shui astrology (Nine House Astrology) in Great Britain and internationally.

My dream is that feng shui and its related practices will become incorporated into mainstream architecture, interior design, town planning and will become an integral part of how we construct our homes to reflect a vision of peace and harmony in all our lives.

1
The Origins of Feng Shui

Feng shui is variously pronounced either 'fong shoy' or 'fung schway', depending on the Chinese regional dialect. The literal translation for 'feng' is 'wind' and 'shui' is 'water'.

The purpose of feng shui is to create a sense of harmony in our environment by harnessing the qualities of these two natural elements in a metaphoric sense. 'Wind' represents breath, energy – a quality that is intangible yet pervading all life and living form. 'Water' represents flow, a journey, luck – it needs to move or else it will become stagnant.

In ancient China, as with many other early cultures, people felt their lives were inexorably linked to the earth and the heavens. Their health, security, wealth and fortune depended on choosing an environment that supported them, together with a belief that the influence of the heavens held in store their destiny or their fate. This early link concerning humanity's position between heaven and earth is best expressed in the classic text the *I Ching*, which originated in China around 3000 BC.

A literal translation of *I Ching* is the Book of Changes, suggesting that humanity exists in a changing world, influenced by Heaven and Earth. The *I Ching* has been used for thousands of years in China, primarily as an oracle for helping make decisions and predictions. The *I Ching* has survived through the dynasties of Chinese history and its metaphoric symbolism underpins the interpretation of fundamental feng shui theory. The *I Ching* is built around eight basic trigrams, which are made up of three broken or unbroken lines placed horizontally above each other. The broken lines suggest the passive, giving nature of earth (yin) whereas the unbroken lines represent the unyielding, driven force of heaven (yang). In Chapter 3 I describe the eight permutations of the trigrams together with their representative symbolism relative to your home.

A trigram

The Form School

Most scholars agree that two principal styles of feng shui developed in China between a thousand and two thousand years ago. The earliest was known as the Form School and its origins can be traced as far back as the Han dynasty (200 BC–AD 200). It was primarily developed in the south-western mountainous region of China in order to locate the most auspicious sites for palaces, dwellings and burial grounds. There is undoubtedly some similarity between understanding the 'energy' of the landscape and understanding the theory of acupuncture which appreciates how 'energy' moves through meridians on the surface of the body. In Form School feng shui, the object is to find a location within the landscape that has benevolent chi energy to benefit the inhabitants. Prevention is an important practice common to both feng shui and acupuncture. The obvious advice is to avoid situations or locations that cause disharmony in the first place.

The Compass School

The Form School was further developed, principally by the work of Yang Yung Sung, who was the principal advisor to the emperor in AD 888 and is now widely respected as the forefather of modern feng shui. His works are regarded as classics and some hundred years later, during the Song dynasty they were adapted by the scholar, Wang Chih, who is attributed as one of the main influences in the formation of what we now call the Compass School of feng shui. This developed in the south-eastern plains region of China, where it was difficult to use the obvious topography of mountains that were the inspiration of the Form School in south-western China. The Compass School incorporates many aspects of the Form School, such as finding a favourable site, having good support behind you (the mountain image from the Form School) and a full appreciation of chi energy. The Compass School is a complex and fascinating science that also incorporates the astrology, fate and destiny of the individual, as well as the location, site and compass direction of the home.

Later in the Song dynasty, a government official known as Cun Guan gave up his work to roam and to travel and further developed his ideas based principally on the Compass School. His work is now regarded as the possible early source of the two styles of feng shui that have now become increasingly popular, not only in the West but also in Hong Kong, Taiwan, Singapore and Malaysia, namely the Eight House system and the Triple Gate or Three Gate system. I will be showing you how to use the basics of the Eight House system in this book, as it forms an integral layer of Compass School feng shui, and you may choose to study this fascinating subject further in the future.

With the growing interest in spiritual development in the West, feng shui has made a timely arrival. The three lines of the *I Ching* trigram, which are central to an understanding of feng shui and many other Eastern traditions, depict three areas of our lives. The top line shows our relationship with heaven – our destiny, our spirituality, our potential. The middle line represents our lives now, how we live and interact in this world. The lower line is representative of our environment, the earth that we live on and the more immediate environment of our home. The theory and practice of feng shui show how these three areas interface, and can give us greater responsibility and freedom as we journey through life.

2

The Principles of Feng Shui

Although this book is designed as a practical introduction to feng shui, it is important to emphasise that knowledge of its underlying principles and theory are fundamental to future appreciation of the subject. To the Westerner, the concepts of chi and yin and yang or the models of the Five Elements and the pa kua may initially seem alien. In much of the Orient, there is a deep-rooted and unspoken appreciation of these terms, which pervade almost every aspect of life.

Whether you practise feng shui, martial arts or Chinese medicine, the basic principles apply: how to prevent problems from occurring, how to bring stability and harmony into play and how to strengthen any inherent weaknesses. In this chapter I will introduce some of the underlying principles of feng shui and encourage you to notice their dynamics in your daily life.

Chi

One of the first basic steps in feng shui is to balance the chi of your home and immediate environment. Chi is 'cosmic breath', a powerful and potent force that can be uplifting and energising. At the same time it can also have negative qualities (poison arrows and sha chi) which can be very disruptive.

How do we know chi is present, how do we know it exists? What are its basic qualities? Given that it is invisible, intangible and changeable, it is not uncommon to associate chi with breath or air, the Wind Element 'feng' in the term 'feng shui'. If we could observe, perceive or feel two elements in the natural world that are closely linked with this association of chi, then I think they would be air and water. A modern interpretation of chi could be the electromagnetic force that binds together cells, molecules and all living matter.

One quality within air is vital, and that is the presence of oxygen. We all know what it feels like to take a bracing walk in the fresh air. We all know how it feels when we have exercised vigorously and our body is well oxygenated. Our chi, our spirit, feels lively, sometimes excited and definitely invigorated. If we sit for a long time in a stuffy room, or sleep in an unventilated room, or work long hours in a poorly oxygenated environment, we are likely to feel tired, despondent, depressed and unenthusiastic. If one factor links the various traditional practices of martial arts or meditation or tai chi or chi kung it is the acquisition of the skill called 'proper breathing'. Other techniques and skills are less important in comparison with this vital discipline. Remember that we can survive much longer without food or water than we can without air – only three or four minutes!

A more tangible way to appreciate the quality of chi in our surroundings is to observe the nature of water, the 'shui' in feng shui. Rather like air, water needs to contain plenty of oxygen to be fresh, alive and stimulating. We all know there is a vast difference between the quality of water drawn from a mountain stream and that which may be found in a dark pond in the corner of a farmyard. The one vital difference is the lack of chi in the stagnant pond. We can begin to appreciate the qualities of chi in our lives and in the environment by taking the example of a spring in the mountains and following its course as the stream on its way down through the plains, to the sea. Beginning with the spring, there is an imagery of brightness, lightness, newness, freshness, vigour and youth. As the water tumbles down the side of the hill in small tributaries, the chi could be described as exploratory, fast, spontaneous and unharnessed. If the same water plunges down a waterfall, its chi is described as unstoppable, defiant, exhilarating and courageous. In pools, in shallow areas, in eddies and in backwaters, these quieter, more still areas would reflect chi that is primarily reflective, indecisive or slow. As the stream forms part of a major river on the plains, the chi has now become much slower and the real spirit of the river at this stage is supportive of its local environment, nurturing and replenishing the thirst of neighbouring fields and communities and livestock. In our landscape we also find ponds, whether they are isolated or form part of the meandering route of a small stream. The kind of chi present can be stagnant, dull and uninviting, or reflective and almost broody.

The most practical way to experience chi is to bring yourself into contact with the natural forces of the elements on a regular basis. This could mean taking a walk when it is windy or stormy, or going for a jog in the rain – if you are willing, let yourself get wet! Go out on a very cold and frosty morning, or experience the mellow stillness of snow when it has settled. Get out in the sunshine and, from time to time, albeit for a short period of time, expose your skin to the sun. Take a walk in the woods or a forest and experience the stillness and the driving chi that sends young pine trees up to pierce the woodland canopy. Go for a walk on the beach, kicking off your shoes and feeling the sand or the pebbles between your toes. Paddle or swim in the sea or a river. Stroll in the hills, or quietly read a book by a river.

Secret Arrows

Like chi, 'secret arrows' are an invisible force. However, this quality of chi can be threatening and dangerous to the well-being of the occupants of a house with this kind of chi aimed at its front door. When we looked at the examples of water in nature, many of them showed its fluid and meandering qualities. However, if you imagine this channelled along a straight line or down a gradient, you would have a completely different mountain of water to deal with. Secret arrows are rather like a hurricane – dangerous, volatile and unpredictable.

Secret arrows generate from many different sources, so locating and dealing with them is the first and the most important step to take in whatever form of feng shui you choose to practise with your home. All feng shui practitioners look out for signs of these secret arrows and, if they are present, then their primary advice is how to offer protection by deflecting them or shielding you from them.

Sha Chi

Whereas secret arrows can be described as active (yang) forms of negative chi, sha chi is usually generated from stagnant (yin) sources and can be just as insidious as over-active secret arrows. Examples could include a derelict site opposite your front door, a piece of wasteland or the local cemetery. Protection by means of screening or deflecting is also necessary in these cases.

Sources of Negative Chi

Straight lines, straight edges and direct channels occur very rarely in the natural world. In modern towns and cities, as well as within our homes, there are numerous straight lines and geometrically sharp angular edges.

To combat these problems, a hedge or a low wall at the front of your property will deal with some secret arrows effectively, but those originating from more distant or taller sources need to be reflected back. The most common 'cure' practised in the Orient is the pa kua mirror. These are octagonally shaped devices with the eight trigrams of the *I Ching* painted on the outer edge or frame, while in the centre a mirror helps to reflect back the poison arrows. These have long been used in China for the protection of the property against poison arrows and are never used inside the home or office.

As you stand in your front doorway, looking out, be aware of some of the factors that can cause secret arrows to be directed toward your front door:

Roads Long straight roads generate plenty of over-whelming chi. If this is aimed directly at your front door, then you need to screen it or deflect it. A gate, a low wall, a fence or planting a hedge could form part of the solution.

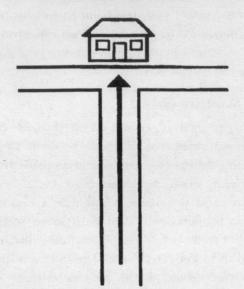

Deflect harmful chi with a hedge or wall

Bridges Bridges are rarely *curved* structures. Bridge crossings generate plenty of chi aimed directly at structures at either end of the bridge. Bridges are always powerful places in the community, highly energised and have always been sought after for their strategic value in warfare.

Paths The path leading up to your front door needs to slow down the chi as it enters your home. A winding, meandering path is ideal, however a front gate that is solid or set slightly to one side of your front door can help slow down the movement of potential secret arrows.

Vehicles Motor vehicles are highly charged. Having one parked directly outside your front door or facing your front door is not ideal. Preferably keep your doorway clear of vehicles, but if this is the only place you can park, then try to reverse into the driveway, leaving the more aggressive forward-facing part of the vehicle pointing away from your front door and property.

Trees Tall and imposing trees within forty metres of your front door can also direct secret arrows in your direction.

Roof Edges The angular corners of buildings opposite your front door can aim secret arrows at you, as can the edges of roofs and gutters pointed in your direction. Recall the images and photographs of traditional roofs in China, where sharp angles are replaced by upturned curves at the edge of the roof, therefore politely deflecting any secret arrows away from neighbours.

Telephone Poles, Utility Poles, Pylons I would not recommend anybody to live close to or under an overhead pylon. There is plenty of evidence to suggest that they generate enormous amounts of negative electromagnetic energy which has the potential to disturb our sleep and, in some cases, has been linked with more serious health problems. Like trees, utility poles facing your front door are sending secret arrows in your direction and they need to be deflected.

Tall, Sharp Structures A church spire, a local sub-station for cellular telephones or a tall radio mast belonging to a local military base, police station or taxi firm can generate powerful energy. If the structure is visible from your front door, this needs to be deflected.

Secret Arrows in the Home Negative chi is also potentially present within our homes. It is wise to try to copy nature by having furniture and structures that 'flow' within our homes. The basic principle to comprehend is that ideally we should use furnishings which lack sharp edges. Notice where you may be threatened by secret arrows generated from the sharp edges of a doorway, a wall, a bookcase or a cupboard, particularly in three important areas: where you sleep, where you work and where you eat. These are three places where you are more likely to spend a lot of your time. Sitting comfortably at your chair in your office, you do not need the sharp angle of a filing cabinet or shelf behind you or beside you deflecting secret arrows in your direction. Similarly, when you are asleep, it is not wise to have the sharp edges of bedside furniture or wardrobes aimed at you while you sleep. Your dining area needs to be free of potential hazards from secret arrows to bring a peaceful and harmonious vibration to where you eat and basically recharge yourself every day. Secret arrows can also be deflected down on us from beams within our property. Ideally avoid sleeping, eating or working underneath such structures. If you have a special chair that you like to relax in after work, then check that you are not sitting under a beam.

Yin and Yang

Yin and yang are expressions of co-existing forces that are opposite yet complementary. In an ideal home environment, you would want to bring in qualities of these two tendencies to create variety, harmony, freshness and inspiration. The basic nature of yin is hidden, dark, still, soft and relaxing, whereas yang is overt, bright, active, hard and energising. Our home is the place where we retreat to recharge, relax, unwind, sleep and eat – all yin activities. Does our environment reflect this, or is it too busy (yang) so that we can never relax? On the other hand, we could overemphasise the yin factors in our home to the point that we only ever ate and slept and never had the energy to circulate, socialise and engage with the outside world.

The Taoist symbolism for yin and yang is represented by the circle which represents a small portion of the opposite quality being held within. This is the perfect way of reminding ourselves that nothing is perfectly yin and nothing is perfectly yang. A small amount of the opposite needs to be represented within it. It also reminds us that there is no such thing as complete balance. In feng shui one of our goals is to create harmony and balance, although we live in a dynamic and complex world and not within a scientifically controlled vacuum.

The Taoist symbol for yin and yang

Yin and Yang Tendencies

Yin's basic nature is to move up and outwards from the earth. This expansive quality generates structures that appear taller, softer, lighter (even hollow) and at the same time create a darker, slower feel.

Yang has its source in heaven. Its energy is directed at the earth bringing focus and clarity while at the same time generating heat, speed and density in its action. Yang structures appear smaller, harder and heavier.

Yin	Yang
Earth	Heaven
Moon	Sun
Shade	Light
Stillness	Movement
Contemplation	Exploration
Slow	Fast
Soft	Hard
Cold	Hot
Water	Fire
Feminine	Masculine
Valleys	Hills, Mountains
North facing (the cold)	South facing (the sun)
Hidden/back	Overt/front

In the Form School of feng shui yin and yang provide the basis for understanding the shape of a structure and its location within the environment. Obvious considerations are whether the structure faces sunshine, whether the building is protected by a hill and whether the building is made of rocks, steel, glass and concrete (yang), or timber or man-made plastic materials (yin).

Yin and yang are also used as a base for interior design. You can bring different colours into the home to represent yin and yang, so that the quality and design of furniture may be light (yin) or heavy (yang), balancing the activities of resting, socialising, cooking, sleeping and work.

The Five Elements

The Five Elements are simply a deeper appreciation of yin and yang. If we were to look at the cycle of change below, then the left-hand part of the cycle would represent the rising energy of yin. As energy beings to 'fall' and return to earth, this is a representation of the yang side of the cycle.

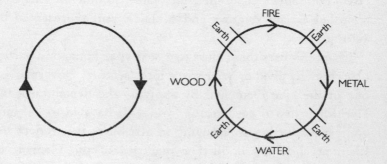

Left, the cycle of change, and right the cycle showing the central role of Earth

The Element Earth is seen as both pivotal and central to the theory of the Five Elements. Originally, its place within this cycle existed between each stage or element.

Applying these elements to the seasons of the year, then summer is reflected by Fire, the gathering energy of autumn is shown by Metal, the reflective still period of winter is represented by Water and the rousing energy of spring is depicted by Wood. Earth was originally represented season-ally as the final few weeks of transition between the end of one season and the beginning of the next. We can all relate to this time of the year where, for example, the change from winter to spring seems to last up to a month. One day we are convinced that spring has finally arrived and the next morning we are disorientated as we are met by flurries of snow or frost on the footpath outside. It is as if the Element Earth acts as a buffer between the seasons.

Nowadays, Earth has its own distinct place within this cycle of the Five Elements, located between Fire and Metal. While Fire continues to represent the summer, Earth is regarded as late summer and Metal is still represented by autumn.

Chapter 4 uses these ideas to assess your home or a partic-ular room by dividing your space into 'sectors' 'governed' by one of the Five Elements. By applying the dynamics of the Five Elements to each sector, you will be able to enhance your space further by bringing in attributes that reflect the Element; bringing in further qualities of the Element to support the Element of the sector; and making sure you do not emphasise an Element that could control or suppress the Element you are trying to enhance.

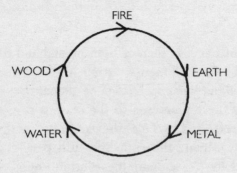

The cycle of elements

The Supportive Cycle

As you look at the cycle of the Five Elements, you will notice that each Element is supported by or mothered by the preceding Element. Water offers nourishment and support to Wood — Water is vital for all plant life. Wood can be represented as any kind of plant life, such as new shoots, bamboo, oak, house plants or massive pine trees. Wood in turn is the mother of Fire. Without the fuel of mature wood, we do not have a fire. The Element Fire is represented by candles, flames, hearths and electric lighting. Fire dies down, to become ashes, and is thus the creator of Earth. Earth or soil is stable, nourishing and rich. Given time and pressure, it consolidates and settles further from ashes through compost, to soil, to hard rock and eventually minerals. Earth is the mother of Metal. The Element Metal can be represented by metallic objects, money or any mineral that is mined. At this stage of the Five Elements cycle, energy is at its most contracted. One of the principles of yin and yang is that, at its extreme point, one will transform into the other. This occurs at this next stage of the cycle, when Metal supports or creates Water — as pressure, heat or time is brought to bear upon minerals, they will melt and this liquid phase or stage is known as Water, which can be represented by ponds, water-falls, fish tanks or water utilities within the home.

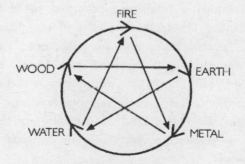

The arrows show the interaction of the elements

The Control Cycle

The illustration on p. 21 shows the internal dynamism of the Five Elements. Each Element has the potential to be over-ridden or controlled by its opposite. As in acupuncture, this really only occurs if one Element becomes far too powerful and therefore imbalanced. In reality, it means that the individual Element concerned fails to support or mother the next Element but instead dashes through to the next stage of the cycle and controls or suppresses the opposite Element instead. In the natural world, we can see this so-called destructive cycle displayed in the following manner:

Wood controls Earth: roots of plants break up soil.
Earth controls Water: earth can absorb or dam the flow of water.
Water controls Fire: water extinguishes fire.
Fire controls Metal: fire melts metal.
Metal controls Wood: metal can cut wood, for example an axe or a saw taken to a tree trunk.

For example, imagine your study or office has an emphasis of the Element Metal. The walls and ceiling are white and other grey or silver decorations or furnishings are also in the Metal spectrum. Metal pieces of furniture — desks, filing cabinets — occupy a small and cramped space along with many mechanical or electrical pieces of equipment such as computers, fax machines and photocopiers. Taken as an extreme example, this overload of Metal energy will suppress the Wood energy of your space. Wood energy can best be described as our creativity, our ideas, our capacity to initiate action, so in this kind of environment the Metal is controlling or stagnating your creative potential. You may feel uninspired.

One solution could be to bring more of the Element Water into play. This helps to 'drain' away excess Metal by drawing from it. At the same time Water will help nurture and feed the suppressed Element Wood. Enhancements might include a strategically placed water feature, a tropical fish tank or a painting that is representative of Water.

Attributes of the Five Elements

Wood

Season:	Spring
Time:	Dawn
Chi:	Uplifting
Age:	Birth
Human activity:	Waking up, feeding, physical exertion
Colour spectrum:	Blue, green
Work activities:	Ideas, initiative
Building shape:	Tall, oblong, vertical
Organs:	Liver, gall bladder
Weather:	Windy

Fire

Season:	Summer
Time:	Midday
Chi:	Expansive
Age:	Pre-pubescent
Human activity:	Travel, going out
Colour spectrum:	Red
Work activity:	Advertising, public relations, sales
Building shapes:	Sharp, pointed roofs, spires
Organs:	Heart, small intestine
Weather:	Very hot

Earth

Season:	Late summer
Time:	Afternoon
Chi:	Settling
Age:	Adolescence
Human activity:	Settling, steady
Colour spectrum:	Yellow
Work activity:	Stability, reinvestment
Building shapes:	Square
Organs:	Spleen, stomach, pancreas
Weather:	Humid

Metal

Season:	Autumn
Time:	Evening
Chi:	Contracting
Age:	Adulthood
Human activity:	Gathering
Colour spectrum:	White
Work activity:	Finances, success
Building shapes:	Round, domes
Organs:	Lungs, large intestine
Weather:	Dry

Water

Season:	Winter
Time:	Night
Chi:	Floating
Age:	Old age
Human activity:	Sleep
Colour spectrum:	Black
Work activity:	Reflection, long-term planning
Building shape:	Low, wavy, long
Organs:	Kidney, bladder
Weather:	Cold, wet

The Pa Kua

The pa kua is another important element of feng shui theory and is deeply embedded in the Compass School of feng shui. The pa kua (also known as the bagua) is an octagonal representation of the eight trigrams of the *I Ching*. The trigrams themselves form part of the calculation used by traditional feng shui masters when looking at the horoscope of a building or a new building site. The pa kua and its relevant 'sector' can also be superimposed over the plan of a city, a building site, a home, a room, a desk or even a business card.

There are two versions of the pa kua.

Earlier Heaven Arrangement

The original layout of the pa kua, reputed to have been drawn up by Emperor Fu Hsi (*c.*3000 BC), sets out the trigrams of the *I Ching* opposite each other.

This is always regarded as the idealised version of the pa kua and is also used as part of the feng shui master's compass.

Earlier Heaven arrangement

This arrangement is always presented in the Chinese protective device known as the pa kua mirror. Available in most Chinatowns, this eight-sided plaque has a circular mirror in the centre surrounded by the trigrams from the *I Ching* as set out in the Earlier Heaven arrangement, and is used to deflect secret arrows. The pa kua mirror needs to be strategically placed on the outside of the property. It is important also to remember that while you are deflecting this kind of energy and protecting yourself, be careful where you aim it – you could bring your neighbour poor fortune.

The Later Heaven Sequence

Most scholars believe that King Wen formulated this version of the pa kua in 1200 BC. The Later Heaven sequence uses the same trigrams from the *I Ching* as the Earlier Heaven arrangement but places them in a sequential order. Essentially, it relates the symbolism of the pa kua to earthly matters and activities and is extensively used in all forms of Compass School feng shui and its related astrology.

The Later Heaven sequence

Remember that when looking at the trigrams on the pa kua, their first line is always positioned nearest to the centre.

Trigrams of the Pa Kua

Each of the sub-sections of the pa kua has its own particular connotations. These include: the symbol of the trigram as represented in the *I Ching*; the family member that they represent; the Element that they reflect in nature; one of the Five Elements; compass directions; seasons; and time of day.

Chien

Symbolism:	Creative
Family Member:	Father
Natural Element:	Heaven
Trigram:	All three lines of this trigram are yang, representing the full masculine influence and presence of heaven and father
Element:	Big Metal
Compass Direction:	North-west
Season:	Late autumn
Time:	Evening, 9.00pm–midnight

Kun

Symbolism:	Receptive
Family Member:	Mother

Natural Element:	Earth
Trigram:	All three lines of this trigram are yin, representing the full presence of earth and the feminine principle
Element:	Big Earth
Compass Direction:	South-west
Season:	Late summer
Time:	Afternoon, 3.00pm–6.00pm

Chen

Symbolism:	Arousing
Family Member:	Eldest son
Natural Element:	Thunder
Trigram:	The yang first line of this trigram pushing upwards towards the two yin upper lines, representing growth.
Element:	Big Wood
Compass Direction:	East
Season:	Spring
Time:	Dawn, 6.00am–9.00am

Sun

Symbolism:	Gentle
Family Member:	Eldest daughter
Natural Element:	Wind
Trigram:	The yin first line of the trigram is pushing upwards towards the two yang lines, symbolic of penetration.

Element:	Small Wood
Compass Direction:	South-east
Season:	Late spring
Time:	Morning, 9.00am–noon

Kan

Symbolism:	Abysmal
Family Member:	Middle son
Natural Element:	Water
Trigram:	The yang middle line of the trigram is surrounded by upper and lower yin lines, representing caution.
Element:	Water
Compass Direction:	North
Season:	Winter
Time:	Night, midnight–3.00am

Li

Symbolism:	Clinging
Family Member:	Middle daughter
Natural Element:	Fire
Trigram:	The one yin line is in the centre surrounded and protected above and below by two yang lines. This trigram represents clarity.
Element:	Fire
Compass Direction:	South
Season:	Midsummer
Time:	Midday, noon–3.00pm

Ken

Symbolism:	Stillness
Family Member:	Youngest son
Natural Element:	Mountain
Trigram:	The first two lines of the trigram are yin and are protected from above by the yang top line. This trigram suggests 'keeping still'.
Element:	Small Earth
Compass Direction:	North-east
Season:	Late winter
Time:	Before dawn, 3.00am–6.00am

Tui

Symbolism:	Joy
Family Member:	Youngest daughter
Natural Element:	Lake
Trigram:	Two Yang lines at the base give way to the softer, gentle yin line above. This trigram suggests joyousness (joy).
Element:	Small Metal
Compass Direction:	West
Season:	Autumn
Time:	Early evening, 6.00pm–9.00pm

The Pa Kua and Your Home

In Chapter 4 you will have the opportunity to superimpose the pa kua over the floor plan of your entire home or each individual room. It is important to align the pa kua with the compass direction of your floor plan to give you eight sectors to work with – remember to get used to working with the idea that South (Fire) is always occupying the top of the pa kua.

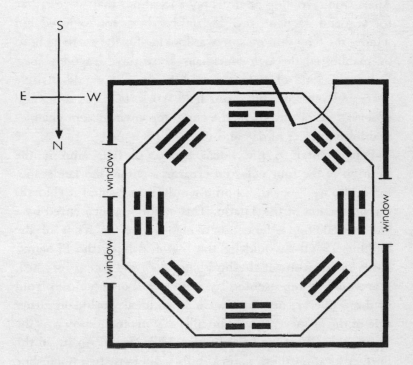

Aligning the Pa Kua with the compass direction of your floor plan

Different Approaches to Feng Shui

The Form School

This is undoubtedly the oldest school of feng shui and was traditionally used to locate the most favourable locations for what are known as yin dwellings (burial sites) or yang dwellings (homes). Feng shui masters would have been taught the art of locating favourable chi from a relative who was an expert or perhaps may have been chosen by a master who sensed they had the potential skill to learn this system. Apart from avoiding obvious poor locations that were either too wet and stagnant, too dry and harsh, or too exposed and windy, the feng shui master was looking for the earth's chi to be manifested through meridians known as 'dragon veins'. Today this kind of approach is difficult as it would involve years and years of study and field work. It requires several observations of the site as the chi of the environment changes at different times of day and night.

Fundamental to the Form School of feng shui is the location of the four celestial creatures within the landscape. In an idealised world, a home would have behind it (North) the protection of the Turtle. This could be represented by a hill, a building, a fence or a high hedge. In front of the building (South) would be the mythical bird, the Phoenix. Hovering in front of the building, alert and facing forward, this would be represented by a lower hill or mound in front of the property, or a low wall. In an ideal world, on either side of the property would be hills that protect, known as the Tiger Hills (West) and the Dragon Hills (East). Again, in the perfect location these natural hills would create a horseshoe encircling the sides and the back of the property. Ideally the Dragon (East) would be slightly higher – in contemporary times this could mean a higher wall or hedge to the left of your property. The Tiger (West) needs to be a lower structure and preferably undisturbed. A contemporary view of the Tiger might suggest 'disturbing it' brings irritation, frustration and anger to the occupants. Neighbours banging on your wall, people throwing litter on the side of your property or children kicking a football against your boundary will all disturb the Tiger!

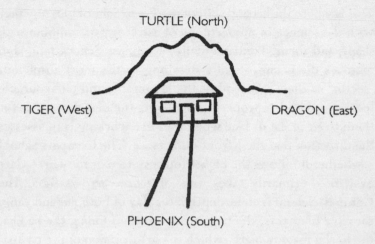

The ideal position of the four celestial creatures around a home

All schools of feng shui aim to ward off secret arrows and look for symbolism of the four celestial animals in the local environment. The basic precepts of the Form School of feng shui are undoubtedly common sense. We would all benefit from an ideal landscape and would feel a subconscious sense of security if we were well protected. Choosing a site that is bright, fresh and alive and that has maintained generations of healthy humans makes sense.

However, hunting for dragon veins at all times of day and night in different seasons and all climates is virtually impossible nowadays. There are few such experts. We live in a culture that puts enormous time constraints on us. Looking for ideal versions and positions of the four celestial animals is also difficult.

The Compass School

This is where the art and skill of the Form School join together with the science of numerology of astrology to combine with shape and form. Fundamentally, Compass School feng shui matches the occupants of a dwelling to the most auspicious 'sector' of their home, plots the favourable and unfavourable locations within a property, highlights the best directions for them to sit or eat or face when they are working, and assesses the direction that their front door faces. The Compass School – whether it follows the Eight House system or the Three Gate System – primarily takes care of secret arrows first. The Compass School is an in-depth interplay of both yin and yang, the Five Elements, the trigrams from the *I Ching*, the pa kua, the lo shu magic square (which is a grid version of the pa kua) and a very detailed approach to traditional Chinese astrology which incorporates the ten heavenly stems (yin and yang versions of each of the Five Elements) and the twelve earthly branches with their associated directions and Chinese zodiacal numbers. These stems and branches combine together to form the twenty-four compass directions of the feng shui expert's lo p'an.

The lo p'an compass is a more detailed and sophisticated development of the pa kua and has between eight and thirty-six concentric rings which help the master to assess the full potential of your home or business.

Compass School feng shui is undoubtedly a remarkable and

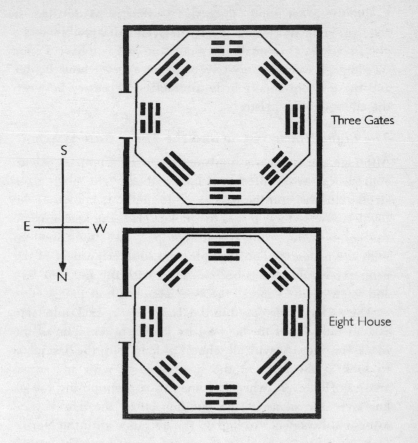

Three Gates

Eight House

The Three Gates and Eight House system

detailed system. With a good teacher and access to plenty of practical study, the basics of this system can be applied. The western mind is not afraid of science, mathematics and patient study. There are no fuzzy edges or hazy interpretations. It is, without a doubt, a science and takes feng shui to deeper levels.

On the other hand, since this system is so detailed, it requires great skill which is only derived from practise and a good teacher. One small miscalculation and you have a poor 'reading'. It can seem mysterious to the average householder and there is potentially little interaction necessary between the client and the master.

The Eight House System and the Three Gate System

Although the pa kua is fundamental to all Compass Schoo. approaches, two different schools of thought now place strong emphasis on the pa kua. One method, known as the Eight House system, places the pa kua grid (the lo shu magic square) over the property with compass directions lined up with the property. For example, the southern aspect of the property would always be associated with the Element Fire and the trigram Li and all the associated symbolism.

The pa kua is also used in the Three Gate, or Triple Gate system introduced to the west by Professor Lin Yun of the Black Hat Sect. As with all schools of feng shui, the first job is to look at the form of the site and deal with any secret arrows. However, when it comes to superimposing the pa kua over the plans of the building, then the Three Gate System always needs to line up the entrance with the North-east, North or North-west sectors of the pa kua. This means that the bottom line of the pa kua needs to be matched up with the entrance to the house or room or even the position in which you sit at your desk, irrelevant of the compass direction.

Both of these approaches have greatly helped to popularise feng shui worldwide over the past thirty years as they simplify feng shui's principles and bring them to a practical level which can be applied by any householder. Without a doubt, the current interest and appreciation of feng shui

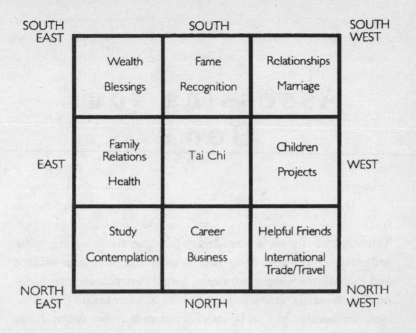

The pa kua grid

would not have been so widespread without the awareness that these two approaches have brought. However, it is possible that these two styles will become so popularised that it will be easy to overlook the fact that they offer only one perspective on a huge subject. Without a doubt, in the right hands, both these approaches have their value.

3

Assessing Your Home

This chapter forms a step-by-step guide to assessing your property. Given that feng shui is such an enormous subject and each of our homes is unique, I shall concentrate primarily on the essentials. It is exciting to look at your home from this new perspective but do be careful not to become dogmatic in your understanding of the ideas that I put forward in the following sections. The approach I use in this chapter can open up into a fuller understanding and appreciation of the Compass School of feng shui and is based on the Eight House Method.

Trust your intuition. The more you delve into the Compass style, the more you will realise that it is a precise and exacting science. The calculations are extremely precise and there is little tolerance for variation. However, as you explore the first levels of the system, use the principles outlined in the following sections to relate the pa kua to your living space but by all means take note of your own intuition when it comes to looking at the enhancements or so called 'cures' you could use. There could be a variety of ways that you could implement cures for bringing stability, for example, into your space. It could involve the introduction of colour schemes, lighting, furnishings, imagery and objects that are symbolic of or represent stability. It is on this level that I encourage you to be intuitive. Go with what you feel is appropriate, based on your taste, style, circumstances and the kind of property that you occupy.

The History of Your Property

Who used to occupy your home? What do you know about them? How was their health? Were they financially successful? The chi that emanates from us and our predecessors has the capacity to 'saturate' the walls of a property. Negative chi present in soft furnishings such as curtains, bed linen and carpets can easily be washed or dry-cleaned. However, when chi energy is absorbed in more solid structures such as masonry, plaster and woodwork, it takes more time and effort to remove them.

On a superficial level, we have all experienced the phenomenon of chi when we have entered a room that has been occupied by a couple of people who were obviously in the middle of an unpleasant discussion moments earlier. We can feel it in the air. We talk about the vibrations that are present. It takes no extraordinary skill to pick up on this kind of chi.

Imagine then, the implications on your space when the habits of a lifetime have saturated themselves within the space. Were the previous occupants worried? Were they under stress? Were they young and healthy? Were they elderly and infirm? Without being aware of it, this chi from the previous occupants can rub off on you also.

Did the previous occupants move on to a bigger and more expensive property because of success at work? If they did, then you have the potential to fall into their slipstream and perhaps pick up on some of the successful chi that they have left behind. If you are a young couple, planning a family, did the previous occupants have lots of healthy children and simply move on to a larger space to accommodate them all? If you are planning to retire soon, did the previous occupants live to a healthy and happy age while occupying the property?

Did the previous occupants have serious health problems? Did they suffer serious injury in an accident? Did they die because of illness they developed while living in the property? Did the previous occupants continually fight and bicker, culminating in separation or divorce? Did the previous occupants have to sell due to financial hardship? Was the house repossessed by the bank or building society?

None of us want to be caught up in the slipstream of any of these events! In Chapter 7, I will touch on the art of 'space clearing', explaining what can be done by a professional to remove the shadow of this old chi from your space if you feel that it is blocking your potential for growth and success.

The Location of Your Property

As objectively as possible, begin to see how your immediate environment reflects on both you and the occupants of your home and the success that you are having. For thousands of years, all over the world, human beings have been drawn to environments that support their health and well-being and at the same time defend them from danger. For example, higher ground was always chosen in favour of marshy land and centres of commerce were always sited close to easy access to the sea or a major river. Modern homes are invariably built on what we call 'green land' or within the 'green belt' but because of the constraints of space, more and more modern properties are being built on so-called 'brown belt' land. This is frequently recycled land which previously may have been a community, refuse dump, or the site of a Victorian industrial factory, for example. Ideally we need a powerful charge from both heaven and earth and we are not going to benefit greatly from siting our home on disturbed and potentially polluted subsoil.

What kind of people are drawn to the area in which you live? Is it predominantly an area populated by families or retired people? Does the neighbourhood attract people who are successful in their work, or are the majority of your neighbours struggling or unemployed? Does the area have plenty of energy representing newness, growth and movement – schools, play areas and sports fields? On the other hand, does the area have many of the more 'yin' attributes that are brought about by the presence of areas of derelict ground, cemeteries or inactive churches?

What is the local crime rate like compared to other districts you have lived in? Have you been burgled since you moved in? Does the whole street have burglar alarms? Are the neighbours friendly, cooperative and sociable? Do you feel isolated and threatened in your neighbourhood?

The Type of Property

Take into consideration the kind of property that you occupy – not so much the shape and size of your home but the type of dwelling it is. There is going to be a difference between living, for example, in a basement, an open-plan loft, a flat in a high-rise building, a terraced house, a detached house, a semi-detached house, a converted barn or a mobile home. If you are living in a basement, basic considerations can help counteract the quality of chi you are likely to experience in this space. You are going to need more light, brightness and enhancers to break up any stagnation that may be present. On the other hand, if you live at the top of a high-rise building, you are going to need some form of 'grounding' to help you keep your feet firmly on the earth.

Applying the Pa Kua to Your Home

We can potentially stimulate our wealth, career and relationships by enhancing various sectors of our home that relate to aspects of the pa kua. The method that I will explain in this section relies on you placing the pa kua over the floor plan of your home, relative to the compass directions – North, South, East and West – and the intercardinal directions – North-east, South-west, South-east and North-west. The advantage of this method is that it can sit comfortably with any deeper studies of Compass feng shui you may choose to pursue in the future. All the traditional approaches to feng shui acknowledge that North is North and South is South.

STEP ONE:

Begin by sketching a floor plan of your home. You need to do this for each floor that you occupy. It does not have to be very accurate but do include openings for windows and note the ways in which the doors are hinged, opening inwards or outwards. If you have a particular room that you wish to concentrate on, such as your study or bedroom, then complete the sketch for this area only. Remember to sketch in your furniture. If you have a garden, then sketch a plan which includes the whole plot, making sure to include all the features such as paths, compost heaps, flowerbeds, trees, seating and any water features.

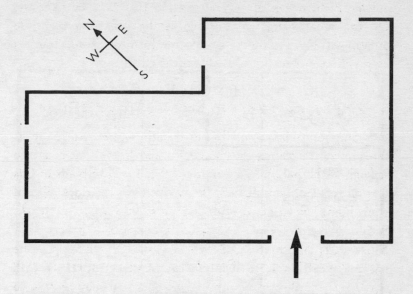

A sample sketch of a home

STEP TWO

Using a simple hand-bearing compass, work out which direction is north and mark out the sectors which represent North, South, East and West and the inter-cardinal points of North-west, South east, South-west and North-east onto the floor plan.

STEP THREE

Square up your space. No plot, house or even room is going to be totally symmetrical. You may find that you have a sector missing in your space or that a projection of your home may be long and narrow, for example, a back kitchen in a typical terraced home or a long extension in a converted stableblock.

Small projections, such as bay windows, porches or

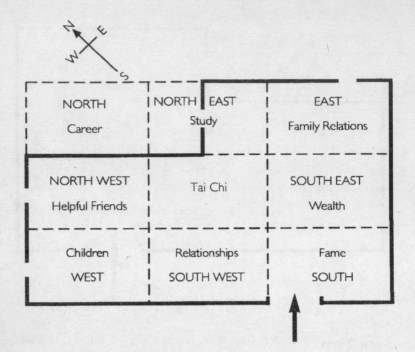

Placing the pa kua over your plan

small conservatories can largely be overlooked while placing the pa kua. However, large extensions that take up 50 per cent or more of a particular side of the home need to be included within the pa kua. You are then likely to be left with a sector or part of a sector 'outside of your home'.

When you align the pa kua over the sketch of your room or plot or entire level of your home, I suggest using a different colour pen to mark in North (career and business), South (fame and recognition), East (family and health), West (children and creativity), North-west (helpful friends, international trade and travel), South-east (wealth and blessings), South-west (relationships and marriage), and North-east (study and contemplation). It is easier to work with at a glance.

STEP FOUR

At this point, be clear about the areas in your life where you are looking to implement change. Does your career need stimulation? Are you having difficulty studying? Are your children doing well at home? How is your relationship with your family?

From the list below, choose a couple of areas that you feel are suitable for development. It is important before setting out on an assessment of your home that you are clear about what you want to achieve. As you begin to instigate changes, this awareness makes the possibility of success with this system even stronger. In my own experience, I have found that it is the intention behind what we do that is very powerful. If we think to ourselves that we may tinker about here and there to see what happens, then the chances of success are limited. Be clear in your mind about what it is you would like to achieve so that you can make changes with that same clarity of purpose.

Career and Business

North How is work at present? Do you feel stuck? Are opportunities coming your way? Are you losing opportunities? Is your career stable?

This area can relate to our 'journey' in life. Do you feel at present that you are aligned with your 'dream'? Do you feel that you are on track with what you really want to be doing with your life?

Fame and Recognition

South Do you feel as if you are being overlooked? This could be at work where your contribution is not being fully appreciated. As a parent, do you feel that your effort is not being recognised? In your community, do you feel as if you are in a backwater?

Do you have a special skill that you wish to be recognised? Have you created a product that needs to be marketed and 'seen'? Are others less talented than yourself, appearing to get the recognition that you feel you deserve? What do you wish to be known for?

Family and Health

East How is your relationship with your parents? Do you have regular communication with them? Are they supportive of what you are doing?

If your mother or father has died, were you in a good relationship with them at the time of their death? Do you feel grateful and inspired by their contribution to your life?

What is your relationship with your boss? Are you being recognised, supported and encouraged?

Children and creativity

West If you have children, how is your relationship with them? Are they succeeding well at school or college? How is their health? Do they need support, inspiration and a little more luck with their examinations?

What are your plans for work and future projects? Are they developing rapidly, or are they on the back burner? Do you need to get these ideas communicated more widely? Do you need inspiration? Do you need motivation in this area?

Helpful Friends, International Trade and Travel

North-west   Are you getting support and love from close friends? Are you getting their advice and guidance? Are you in good communication with your neighbours? How is your phone system? Business high-flyers reported to have sought advice from feng shui experts include Donald Trump and Richard Branson.

If you are in business, how are sales developing abroad? Do you wish your products to be marketed internationally and are you prepared to travel overseas to initiate these sales?

Wealth and Blessings

South-east   How is your luck at present? Do you feel that opportunities are coming your way, or are you being over-looked and left out? Are you looking for promotion at work?

How is your financial situation? Do you have adequate savings for the future? Do you have good cash flow?

Are you open to receiving spontaneous opportunities that can bring you luck and prosperity?

Relationships and Marriage

South-west   Are you in a relationship at present? If so, is it happy and harmonious and going the way you want? Is there stability in the relationship? Does it have good communication?

If you are not in a relationship at present, do you wish to be? If so, how do you see that relationship?

How are your relationships with work colleagues, old friends, neighbours, clients? Is there harmony and balance?

Study and Contemplation

North-east Do you need more time and space for your own self-development? Are you so busy with your career and family life that your spirit is being neglected?

Are the demands on your time at work such that you have little time for yourself? If you are a student, are you finding yourself distracted? Are you looking for consistency, stability, inspiration or motivation in your studies?

Now prioritise a couple of areas where you wish to implement change.

1 _____

2 _____

The Eight Sectors

Once you have achieved a clear sense of what you are looking to undertake with your feng shui project, check the relevant part of your home and then refer to the suggestions that I outline for each sector. These sectors could be represented over the entire plot, including the garden, a whole floor or level of your property or an individual room.

For example, if what you would like to achieve in the coming months is better concentration in your studies, you will obviously choose to look at the sector or sectors that represent study and contemplation which occupy the North-east sector of your property, garden or individual room. If you have been feeling too distracted or have felt too restless or lack the motivation, then check these north-east sectors to see how they may reflect how you are 'stuck' at present. Make changes that would foster clarity, focus and a sense of order. Hints and tips would be provided for each sector as you go through.

'Less is More'. If many of the areas in your life in the list above are already working satisfactorily, then don't tinker with them. It is fine to make a few small adjustments here and there to bring stability or more energy into a certain area of life. Attempting to bring about changes in all these areas when many of them seem reasonably satisfactory is going to cause far more of an upheaval.

North

Subsection: Kan (water)
Element: Water
Sector of the pa kua: Career and business
Water symbolism in this sector of your home can be interpreted as the winding path or journey of your career. Its successful, flowing and enjoyable aspects can be mirrored in this particular sector. The imagery of the Element Water can also represent financial success and rewards from your career. Is it flowing? Is it stuck? Do you need more?

Support for this Sector   Colours that represent North and Water are best if they are darker, especially with blue present. A water feature in this sector may be appropriate. A stagnant fish pond in this sector of your garden, however, does not represent a flowingly successful career! Bright, fresh, well oxygenated water with healthy fish could be of benefit.

If you do choose to include a water feature in this sector within your home, make sure that it fits in 'proportionally' with the rest of your space. Also, do not be tempted to over-activate it by having a fountain shooting up several feet, as this can lead to an erratic nature within your career – too many opportunities and perhaps too many lost opportunities. Images of flowing water in the form of artwork would be excellent. Meandering rivers and gentle oceans, seascapes or even images of fish are fine, but thundering storms hitting an isolated lighthouse on a rock are not necessarily what you should have in mind.

If This Sector is Missing   In Chinese medicine, Water represents the health and vitality of our kidneys, bladder and reproductive system and gives us our vitality. With this sector missing, you could easily become tired, run down and withdrawn.

If This Sector is Extended   Water provides us with enormous capacity for reflection and intuition. An intuitive approach to your career could make you extremely successful – especially financially.

If Your Front Door Faces North   This sector can re-present winter and you may have a tendency to feel cold, isolated, withdrawn or threatened. Overall, it is not an ideal direction as traditionally chill winds approach you from this sector. You could well end up 'hibernating' in this situation!

South

Subsection: Li (fire)
Element: Fire
Sector of the pa kua: Fame and recognition
Fire is an extremely powerful element. Its imagery brings with it a sense of brilliance, clarity, perception, intuition and wisdom and it has the capacity to cut through delusions and

help to bring clarity to all around. Fire in this sector represents recognition and acknowledgement for what you have achieved. You can enhance what you have been known for and what you would like to be known for by using this sector of your space appropriately.

Support for This Sector   In terms of the colour scheme, Fire represents the colour red and various shades including purple, pink and maroon. It also represents brightness, so make sure that the colours in this sector are fresh and bright and not lacklustre. Fire is also represented by light. Make sure that this sector is well lit. You may even choose to include real fire in the form of candles.

Place some representation of what you want to be known for within this sector. Perhaps this is a diploma from college or a trophy or a work of art that you have created and are proud of. It is also best to limit your desire for recognition and fame to a particular area, rather than have several represented in this sector. Fire, after all, is about clarity.

Plants positioned here will thrive well since they are facing the sun. Also, Wood energy is the mother of Fire and is supportive of this sector.

If this Sector is Missing   A lack of recognition, acknowledgement or success is bound to leave you feeling low in self-esteem and confidence.

If this Sector is Extended   You will be famous! It offers great potential for success, recognition and wisdom.

If Your Front Door Faces South   Fire is always going to activate whatever is present. If you put a bright light in a dusty corner, it doesn't make it less dusty, it makes it look worse! If you are unhappy and low in self-esteem, it is only going to magnify and activate these feelings. Fire also charges the atmosphere. This could lead negatively to arguments for the occupants.

On the positive side, remember that the energy of Fire will undoubtedly activate the house and its occupants, making them more fun, lively and sociable.

East

Subsection: Chen (thunder)
Element: Wood
Sector of the pa kua: Family and health
East and the dawn represent our health and our vitality. They also represent our family, parents, ancestors and elders and it can encompass other 'senior' members of our circle, such as a boss. In a traditional sense, it can represent the 'tribe' to which we belong. A modern understanding of this could be that as individuals we are each members of several different tribes — a work tribe, a family tribe, a recreational tribe (eg. yoga class, golf club), our studying tribe, and so on.

Support for This Sector The dawn, spring and the beginning of a cycle, in combination with Wood, can be influenced and stimulated by fresh, lively, tall green plants. You are not looking for drooping, heavy, downward energy in this sector. This is a very energised and energising sector of your home. Remember that the creator of Wood is Water so it may be appropriate to have a small water feature in this sector. Obviously the colours of spring, such as green and various hues of blue, would be beneficial. The imagery of freshness and beginnings are also appropriate.

Photographs and images of your 'tribe' could be represented here too. However, if they are photographs of parents and ancestors who have died, make sure that these photographs or paintings are small. Try and remember the feeling you had when you last visited a castle, country mansion or art gallery which had large wall-to-wall portraits of previous occupants staring down at you. It is not an energising atmosphere.

If This Sector is Missing   As this area represents the full force of spring, then obviously a missing portion will leave the occupants low in stamina. The occupants may also feel out of touch with their parents, their boss or their 'tribe'.

If This Sector is Extended   This is very beneficial for all occupants, bringing great health and vitality especially.

If Your Front Door Faces East   Facing the east brings the new energy of dawn into the home. This is a very auspicious direction for new developments, starting a career and for the growth of an existing business. The symbolism of dawn and new life is particulary beneficial to children who occupy this home.

West

Subsection: Tui (lake)
Element: Metal
Sector of the pa kua: Children and creativity
This is especially good for young people and the new shoots of your family, your children. It is also excellent for growth, new careers and new possibilities and developments. Associated with warmth, communication and fun, it is also the space for inspiration. It is a place that fires up our imagination for future projects, schemes and dreams. This area represents our creativity, our projects and of course our 'children'.

Support for This Sector   How is your social life? Is your creativity or your imagination a little bit jaded at present? How is the health, well-being, creativity and academic success of your children at present?

To bring a charge to this sector of your home, emphasise the sensory aspects of this area. Ideally, this sector needs to be comfortable, warm and relaxing. Whites and off-whites are the ideal colours. Include paintings, gifts and trinkets that represent relaxation, imagination and creativity. This could be the sector of your home or room where you keep your stereo system.

If This Sector is Missing   It could be difficult for the occupants to conceive. If they do have children, they may have difficulties with them. Since this sector represents aspects of our social life, it could mean that the occupants feel isolated socially. Metal is the Element of this sector and this could result in an instability with cash flow, and never having enough money to meet all your needs.

If This Sector is Extended   The occupants can be very active socially, both at home or away from the home. Parties would tend to be memorable! The occupants' children would be very active, especially socially, and other neighbourhood children would be attracted to the space. There would be plenty of phone calls, parties and sleep-overs.

If Your Front Door Faces West   There is potential here for a generous income matched with equally demanding outgoings. This is a bright, happy home with plenty of fun, frivolity and romance.

North-west

Subsection: Chien (heaven)
Element: Metal
Sector of the pa kua: Helpful friends, international trade and travel

Sitting diagonally across from the South-east sector of your space, which represents wealth and blessings, is the North-west sector, representing helpful friends. Their polarity presents a good example of yin and yang – giving, as well as receiving. Stimulating this sector of your home can bring about good relations with your neighbours, or contact with old friends and mentors. If you feel out of touch, lack of support or are not receiving enough enquiries regarding your work, then you should focus on this sector.

Ask yourself how much support you give to your neighbours and your community. Put aside time every week where you give your energy unconditionally in some form of charitable project. Donating your time to others will benefit you equally in the support that you receive.

You should also stimulate this sector if you wish to have your horizons widened with travel or international trade.

Support for This Sector   Chien represents the full force of heaven – yang. Colours that represent this trigram include all shades of white including cream, silver and grey. Solid, 'metallic' objects bring focus and clarity to this area. These can include lead crystal and the most valuable yang minerals on earth – diamonds.

To stimulate international trade and travel and your relationship with other parts of the world, why not include a globe in this sector? To give it added stimulus, find one that lights up within. In this day and age, our communication with the outside world is inevitably through the telephone, the fax and the Internet. This could well be the sector of your home or study where you position your communication centre.

If This Sector is Missing   Given that this sector is represented by the full force of yang – the male principle – then men will be affected more adversely if this sector is missing. They could suffer from poor communication and a lack of support from friends, mentors and colleagues, and in addition they may lack the full charge of yang, leaving them low in energy and stamina and prone to low-grade health problems.

If This Sector is Extended   This translates as having too much yang which, far from being beneficial, could actually be detrimental. Too much yang could represent lack of support and a feeling of isolation.

If Your Front Door Faces North-west   The representation of heaven, father and the male principle means that a door in this sector is very auspicious for the male members of the household. 'Heaven' entering into this sector stimulates the presence of 'Father', bringing the male household respect and trust in the eyes of the community and work colleagues.

South-east

Subsection: Sun (wind)
Element: Wood
Sector of the pa kua: Wealth and blessings
The South-east sector brings the symbolism of warmth and the blossoming of energy. On a seasonal level, it represents the late spring when plant life is at its most abundant. This is a very powerful sector of your home that brings with it not just the potential for financial prosperity but also good health

and luck, so enhancing this area of our home can really help to make miracles happen. So much success in terms of work or wealth is often about being in the right place at the right time. Keeping this sector bright and fresh gives you a doorway into opportunity.

If you are feeling particularly down on your luck, are missing opportunities or have irritating health problems, then it is vital that you check this area for stagnation. This is not the area for your rubbish bins, clutter or your toilet!

Support For this Sector   The element wood is represented in this sector and it can be stimulated by the presence of healthy, vibrant plants. This is a popular sector to enhance by the use of a money tree, also known as the jade plant or Crasulla, a slow-growing succulent with rounded leaves that needs very little water but plenty of sunshine. The bigger the better and they are all the more auspicious if they flower once or even twice a year.

In the Five Elements cycle, Water promotes and supports Wood. A small water feature in this sector could also be of value.

For colour schemes, look at the range that includes shades of blue and red, including blue, mauve, purple and burgundy.

If This Sector is Missing   Without the support of this sector within your home or room, then you may well find yourself facing financial problems and being generally out of luck. Others around you may seem to have miracles happen for them whereas you are left on the sideline. Since this area also represents money in terms of wealth, you may well find yourself having continued financial worries and even possibly legal problems draining your resources.

If this Sector is Extended Here you have the opportunity for enormous success, luck, prosperity and vibrant health. Opportunities could literally overwhelm you. However, you need to be cautious not to overcommit yourself in too many directions.

If Your Front Door Faces South-east The chi entering your home from the South-east will make it a very vibrant, happy and active space. This is excellent for maintaining contacts and good communication with the outside world, leading to new projects and endeavours. Initiating and undertaking new ventures will seem effortless, though you may need to put aside some time and energy in order to see them through to their completion.

South-west

Subsection: Kun (earth)
Element: Earth
Sector of pa kua: Relationships and marriage
Traditionally, this sector of your home was synonymous with marriage. In this day and age, it can have a wider understanding to include not only your relationship with your partner but also your relationships with colleagues at work, neighbours and your family. Check this sector to see how it mirrors your relationship – or lack of relationship – at present.

The symbolism of the full force of earth, as represented by the trigram Kun, is that of receptivity. This is the most yin, or open, of all the trigrams. This is not a sector of your home in which to have a filing cabinet filled with old magazines and correspondence, for example. If you are looking to start a new, fresh relationship, then it is not the place for a momento of a previous love dominating the space. This is the sector that is about being open to and receiving a relationship in your life.

Support for this Sector The full force of earth in this sector can be stimulated by the use of crystals, which represent this element. Remember also that Fire supports earth in the Five Elements and the use of real fire — a fireplace or, more easily, candles — can be beneficial. The hole layout of this sector needs to be warm, inviting and cosy. Colours that are light shades of red are beneficial — pinks, blossoms and off-whites with a tinge of red.

The imagery of relationships in this sector is also important. A photograph of you and your spouse at a very happy time in your life is ideal. Paintings that depict people or even animals in pairs can subliminally suggest 'relationships'. What you obviously want to avoid are images of you in isolation. Furnishing and seating should be cosy and comfortable.

If This Sector is Missing This sector is charged by the full force of yin which is the feminine principle. With this sector missing, the female occupants of the house are going to feel far more uncomfortable than the men. The potential for the natural charge of yin is going to be restricted, leaving feelings of discomfort, isolation and possible health problems.

If This Sector is Extended Women are going to feel particularly happy and comfortable in a home that has a larger South-west aspect. Generally, the home will have a feeling of warmth and relaxation and receptivity to others. A happy, calming influence will pervade.

If Your Front Door Faces South-west This sector of your home receives the benefit of the energy brought with the late afternoon. This is a mellow time when the chi of the Earth settles and begins to consolidate. With the front door in this sector, the occupants will feel warm, supported and content but retiring. This slowing down is also emphasised in the strong yin factor represented by the trigram Kun. This could be an ideal home for a happy couple embarking on a long and mellow retirement.

North-east

Subsection: Ken (the mountain)
Element: Earth
Sector of the pa kua: Study and contemplation

The trigram Ken represents the Mountain, which is always symbolic of stillness and contemplation. Ideally, this sector of your home would be best used as your study. The focus of this room is about knowledge, self-reflection and meditation. In an ideal world, this is your quiet haven. With a large family this may well be the space where a child who is sitting their exam can sit to be quiet and inspired as they study.

Support for This Sector   If a room in the North-east sector of your home cannot be a dedicated study then simply be aware of the North-east sector of the room where you have your desk. Bring into this sector images of stillness, such as examples drawn from nature – a winter scene, a mountain or a landscape that inspires you. Darker colours, including dark blues, darker shades of green and small amounts of black are excellent within this space. Empty vases, empty decorative bowls and empty trinket boxes are symbolic of receptivity, which comes with the practice of contemplation. These could be placed on or near your desk in the North-east sector. Remember that the Element Fire supports Earth and you may want to look at the use of candles in this sector, or a bright uplighter instead.

If This Sector is Missing   As this area is associated with contemplation and stillness you may be left with much stronger feelings of isolation. The danger is that you might become too withdrawn. Other members of the household will feel much the same.

If This Sector is Enlarged   In this situation, individual members of the household or family may get too isolated in their own work, projects, activities or social life to really interact effectively with the other members. This will undoubtedly lead to poor communication within the household. When this sector is over-emphasised in this way it shows that the occupants of the home are deep within their Mountains. This means they are likely to have difficulty in being heard, while at the same time it is challenging for them to communicate with others.

If Your Front Door Faces North-east   The most threatening cold winds always come from the North-east. You open the door to a Siberian gale! Strong penetrating yin from the North-east is likely to affect everyone in the home, especially in winter when it can lead to health problems such as colds, chest infections and lingering flu. It is also quite possible that women might find it difficult to conceive in this situation.

The Centre

While this sector does not have specific cardinal directions eg. North, South, North-east, North-west etc., it does play a significant role within your space. The centre is best depicted by the imagery from China of tai chi, or the interpretation of unification (see page 17).

The centre corresponds to harmony and balance within your home. In fact the other eight sectors all interplay and inter-relate through this central section. In an ideal world, you should keep this central aspect of your home or room free of any major pieces of furniture and especially any unwanted clutter. Chi energy needs to flow unhindered through this space, allowing possibility to unfold, and blocking this portion of your room or home can have a detrimental effect on all or any of the other sectors involved.

The only occasion that you may consider having a focal point at the centre of this space would be if there is a major distraction of either sha chi entering the room through a large window, or light or noise coming through the window. On a subliminal level, when you enter the room, rather than being drawn to the distraction outside, your attention could be focused on the centre of the room in a more creative and helpful way. Naturally, only furniture with round features, such as a low, round coffee table, should be placed at the centre. Since the element associated with tai chi is Earth, you could place an ornament symbolic of this element, such as a crystal or an ornamental cut-glass object. Colours that support this central sector would be the various shades of yellow, including light brown, orange and in particular gold.

Clutter

Before getting down to the exciting and potentially life-changing process of bringing feng shui adjustments into your home, it is vital that you clear the way for these changes to occur. Hanging a well-intentioned crystal in the window of your room to bring a bigger and brighter charge to your relationships corner could potentially make your problem worse until you have cleared the stagnation. Many of the adjustments that you can make to enhance the chi in your home will readily enhance the vibration that is already present. If you have found that the sector that you need to work on has piles of old books and photographs and dusty correspondence, then simply placing a crystal in this area is only going to emphasise and enlarge the problem. Before putting any ideas and suggestions into practice, take time to reflect on how you need to prepare your home.

Clutter can be defined as possessions that you don't use any more or no longer love. These are often possessions that we believe may one day be useful, broken items that one day we intend to repair, spares that we accumulate for a potential breakdown, unfinished projects and unwanted gifts. Everything that we own has its own vibration and is energetically connected to us.

There are three kinds of clutter.

Physical Clutter

This relates to the mess and jumble that can accumulate in our homes. Begin by deciding what you really need to keep and what you need to store and what you need to get rid of. On a practical level, keep what you need on a daily basis as simple as possible. Store away items of clothing that are only used seasonally. Be ruthless about getting rid of what you really do not need. Since every possession we own has its own vibration, think carefully before you pass it on to a neighbour. Do you really think they need it? Charity shops and recycling centres can make good use of your unwanted jumble.

I encourage you to keep the entrance to your home a clutter-free zone. Remember that it is through this 'mouth' that new opportunities and fresh chi enter your space. Paths, doorways and entrance halls need to be free-flowing to allow access of new chi into your life. If you share a hallway with another neighbour, then be responsible for keeping it clean. If you have asked them for cooperation before and it is not forthcoming, then simply take charge. It only takes a moment to pick up those unwanted flyers that come through the letterbox.

It is vital to keep the kitchen clutter-free too. Pay particular attention to the fridge and make certain that you regularly check every recess for old and out-of-date food. Get behind the cooker from time to time, and have a good clean around the edges. The one area I love to check is the cupboard under the sink! Given that the kitchen is the source of the creation of our health through the daily preparation of our food, then it is a paradox that this same important space can also harbour agents of death and destruction! Heavy-duty bleaches, disinfectants, ant powders, wasp sprays and other potentially hazardous chemicals need to be kept out of the kitchen, which is a vital centre for your health and well-being.

Do check the bedroom for clutter! Out of sight is definitely not out of mind. Stuffing everything into wardrobes and drawers does not simplify the problem as the stagnant and disturbed chi is still present. Be ruthless and decide what is useful, what is storage and what needs to go to the jumble sale. The very worst place to store your clutter is under your bed. It has potential to disturb your sleep and attract dust and mites – it needs removing today!

Finally, go through your desk and filing cabinet. Get rid of those notes and scraps you think may one day be useful and keep everything current and useful. Having dustbins or waste baskets in every room is not a problem, provided you empty them frequently.

Vibrational Clutter

This kind of clutter relates to the negativity we can accumulate when we have unresolved issues surrounding us in our lives. It is insidious, and has enormous potential to block your progress. It may be as simple as an unfinished conversation. Pick up the phone and deal with it. Are there unpleasant rumours or gossip circulating about you at present? If so, do what is necessary to resolve the situation. Have you recently broken an agreement or have somebody renege on their agreement with you? If so, do your best to tackle it as soon as possible. Do you owe anybody anything? If it is a financial debt, then make very clear your proposed plan to settle it. Have you borrowed something and not returned it? Do you have a pile of unanswered letters on your desk? If just looking at them disturbs your chi, then you know you have a problem. What about those messages accumulating on your answerphone? What are you doing about responding to them?

On a subconscious level, this kind of clutter definitely brings a sense of disorder into your space. Put aside a few hours to do your very best to resolve these outstanding issues. Once the 'blockage' is removed, then it allows new possibilities to arrive.

Internal Clutter

This third quality of clutter is related primarily to our current health, and in particular to our digestive system. In Chinese medicine, the Element Metal governs the function of the lung and large intestine. Both of these organs are connected with accumulation, absorption and elimination.

The lungs (yang) are highly charged and active organs connected with the assimilation of the yin element oxygen. Their partner, the large intestine (yin), is connected with the assimilation of solids (yang). When these organs are functioning well we feel positive and energised in our outlook. However, if they become weak or stagnant, we easily reflect this by becoming despondent and depressed. A sense of hopelessness and lack of motivation is one of the key symptoms.

Fresh air and plenty of exercise help to stimulate the lungs and introducing fresh plants into your environment brings with them a freshly oxygenated atmosphere. Getting things 'off your chest' is also vital for the well-being of the lungs. Making your feelings known, letting go of old resentments and not smoking all support the healthy function of the lungs. For the colon, avoid eating late at night (eat at least two hours before you go to sleep) and chew your food very well, as the digestive process begins with the initial breakdown of the food in your mouth by saliva. Avoid overeating and reduce the consumption of heavy baked flour products such as flans, pies and pastries.

Preventing Clutter

Once you have effectively cleared the clutter in your home, what can you do constructively to prevent it from recurring again? The best advice is to have a periodic spring clean. A change of season is always the best time, though the most powerful time would naturally be the spring equinox. Make your spring clean a special occasion. Try not to regard it as a chore but as a ritual that will become part of your life. A deep cleanse of your space will also have a profound effect on your own chi, promoting new ideas and inspiration as well as physical changes in your well-being. Initially you may feel a little tired, stiff and irritable, but these cannot be regarded as side effects of the elimination process. Put aside the requisite amount of time that you know the job will take and avoid being distracted or disturbed – make it a meditation. Once each room is 'declared' clean, emphasise this by lighting a candle, or placing a vase of freshly cut flowers in a favourable position.

Another aspect of prevention is to question items that you are going to buy and bring in to your home. What purpose do they really serve? Are they going to be useful? Are they likely to become clutter in the near future? The dynamics of yin and yang would suggest that when you let go of something you create the opportunity for new possibility. Do you feel guilty about taking a carboot load of junk to your local dump and coming back with a couple of useful items that you found there?

Remember that clutter attracts clutter. Do you recall as a child that you would never dream of walking across your mother's newly washed or polished kitchen floor? And how many times have we visited friends' newly carpeted homes and asked whether we should remove our shoes? However, it is not uncommon when we enter an untidy space that we give little thought to whether we are making the situation worse. Even walking down the street we should always look for a rubbish bin to get rid of that disused bus ticket. But how often are we tempted to dispose of it on top of another pile of rubbish if we can't find a litter bin? We might not throw it in the street but we are certainly tempted to throw it where there is more clutter.

Do be aware of accumulating other people's clutter on their behalf. Friends often ask if they can store a couple of boxes of books while they go away or move house. Before long, a few weeks or months can run into a year or more. Do you really need their clutter as well as your own to contend with? Equally, do you have clutter accumulated at someone else's home? The favourite place to check is your parents' attic, basement or garden shed. What effect is your clutter having on their lives? If any of the issues in this section apply to you, then try to resolve the situation soon.

An interesting case history involves Peter, a journalist who left full-time employment with his magazine to go freelance. The only offers of work that came his way were from the magazine on a part-time basis. It was useful income, but it was not bringing him the stimulus that a new change could have provided.

When he looked in the sector of his office that related to wealth and blessings, lo and behold, there in the corner, piled from floor to ceiling, were his old files and work that he had done for the magazine. He had thought he would go through it all one day to keep the useful and relevant sections. The suggestion was 'clear this up immediately!' The very next day he got a call, right out of the blue, from a completely new client. This simple action of clearing clutter helped move on his work, creativity and chi.

4

Feng Shui
Remedies

As you begin to work your way through your home, there are a few valuable hints and tips to be drawn from the traditional and modern feng shui toolkit. Initially, decide clearly whether you need to instigate any changes at all and if so, need they be of a protective nature, an enhancement, a stimulation or a stabilisation. Do take the precaution of not overdoing the job! Once you have taken care of any cutting chi (poison arrows) outside and inside your property and dealt thoroughly with the issue of clutter, it is only then that you can consider introducing these more subtle remedies.

After attending a fascinating and dynamic presentation on feng shui several years ago in London, I rushed home and made a list of what I needed to instigate. The next day I purchased and placed seven strategically positioned mirrors and four multi-faceted crystals in various windows. Given that it was such a small home, I had really overheated and overcharged the space. Opportunities in my career began taking off instantly. However, at the same time I had to replace four light bulbs – all of which popped within twenty-four hours of placing the cures! Always make any of these changes carefully and with a clear intention of what you wish to achieve. It is no good simply hanging a crystal and hoping. It is far better that you have a clear picture of what you wish to achieve and to be conscious of this while you place the remedy. Always choose a remedy relative in size to the space where you are utilising it. A tiny crystal placed in the window of a cathedral-sized loft would have little effect and similarly a crystal the size of a grapefruit in the window of a small room would have an overbearing effect.

Protection

External

Not every home needs the potent protection of the pa kua mirror (page 26) as these are only intended to deflect sha chi from entering the home through the front door. If you feel that this device is out of place in your neighbourhood, then try using a three- or four-inch highly polished convex mirror placed close to the front door and aimed in the direction of the source of sha chi. A modern device could be a highly polished door knocker. The colour red in feng shui is always associated with happiness, warmth, strength and fame as well as protection, and so you can use this colour to protect your home. The only time a bright red door would be inappropriate would be if it was 'facing' its own source — South (Fire) — as it would have counter-productive effects.

The symbolic use of guardians on either side of your door could also be employed. Many Chinese temples have statues of lions either side of the entrance. Many other cultures have also picked up on the important symbolism of protection offered by these animals. Ideally make sure that if you have a pair of guardians that they are not too large or draw too much unnecessary attention towards your property. Several properties that I have visited have had a pair of watchful owls on the gateposts, symbolic of keeping a watchful eye for intruders.

Internal

A simple way to deflect sha chi entering your home from neighbouring sources through windows can be to hang a smooth, shiny reflective silver ball in the window. This can be hollow or solid, no smaller than a golf ball and hung slightly above your direct eyeline so that it does not draw your attention every time you enter the room. To make a section of your home 'disappear', such as an inauspiciously located toilet, you could hang a full-length mirror on the outside door of the toilet. It can give the illusion that this space does not exist. In the same way, an unwanted sharp-edged supporting pillar in your home could be made to disappear by facing all four sides with a length of mirror. Alternatively, you could 'hide' the pillar by training a plant or creeper around it.

Enhancements

Having decided which sector of your home or individual room represents the aspect of your life that you wish to improve, the following list of enhancements have the potential to strengthen the chi in the relevant sector. Before placing any of these enhancements, always remember that they are designed to support either the Element relevant to the sector or its previous (or supporting) Element within the Five Element cycle. For example, if you wish to stimulate your wealth and blessings sector (South-east), then plants would be an enhancement since its element is Wood. Wood energy supports Fire energy and so the placement of plants in the South sector would also be helpful if you wish to achieve fame and recognition.

Lights

Fire is a microcosm of the sun and bringing this kind of charge into your home and your garden will uplift your environment. Any kind of light is symbolic of the element of Fire. Electric lights, candles, chandeliers, crystals, uplighters and even mirrors all fall into this category. Ideally these are placed in the South sector but can also be utilised in the North-east and South-west sectors. If the South sector of your home is unusually dark and this is currently being reflected in a lack of recognition for your work, then keep the area brightly lit, especially during working hours. To really enhance the sector using lighting, consider the use of an uplighter, which has the added benefit of raising the chi upwards compared with a small, low-wattage table lamp in that sector. If you do use multi-faceted crystals, mirrors, or cut-glass chandeliers, make sure that they are kept very, very clean.

Plants

Any kind of fresh plant life represents Wood. It is best placed in the South-east or East sectors (Wood) or the South sector (Fire). The best representations of Wood energy are either freshly cut flowers or a healthy green plant. Cut flowers are always given as a gift to cheer a person up or make them feel better if they are in hospital. They can hold their freshness for several days but they are best disposed of as soon as they show signs of wilting. Silk imitations of flowers or plants are far better than the dead energy that is associated with dried flowers.

If you are looking to stimulate the South-eastern sector (wealth and fortunate blessings), then perhaps look no further than the money tree (jade plant or Crassula). These slow-growing and hardy succulents often spotted in your local Chinese restaurant, have either round or pear-shaped leaves and are very easy to grow from cuttings. They need very little water but plenty of light and they should be allowed to winterise – give them very little water in the winter. The older and bigger they are, the more likely they are to blossom – perhaps even twice a year, which symbolises success in this sector. To really stimulate this area, the bigger the plant, the better.

Most evergreens and ferns have an ionising effect on the atmosphere while others, including the poinsettia, the peace lily, the ivy and the spider plant are all capable of removing chemicals and toxins from the atmosphere.

Water

A water feature in your home or garden can be an extremely valuable asset, especially if it is placed in either the North, East or South-east sectors. Fresh, clean, sparkling water is symbolic of good health, good chi, good cash flow and a lack of stagnation in your career. Any kind of water feature within your home needs to be proportionate in size to the room that it is in.

You might choose a healthy aquarium with tropical fish such as the sail fin mollie, ideally nine of them (eight red ones and one black one if possible). Remember that male sail fin mollies are aggressive towards each other and if they start breeding you are not going to have your lucky number nine present any longer! Multiples of nine are also fine. A goldfish bowl with odd numbers of healthy goldfish works as well. If you absolutely detest the idea of a fish tank, then fish or water could be symbolised, for example by placing an odd number of ornamental fish in a glass bowl or dish in this sector.

A trickling water feature can also be excellent, but keep the flow of water to a pleasant trickle rather than a gushing fountain. Make sure that the size of this feature is proportionate to the size of your room. Fountains and ponds in your garden are excellent enhancers. Japanese koi are particularly auspicious in ponds, but do keep them protected from your neighbourhood heron. It is also not uncommon in Chinese restaurants to see a small water feature close to the till, symbolising of good cash flow and success in business.

Heavy Objects

Heavy objects symbolise enhanced stability and are best placed in sectors that are represented by Earth (South-west and North-east) or in the Element that they support, Metal (West or North-west). This imagery of stability reinforces and enhances Earth. Statues and heavy earthenware vases, ideally at ground level, are the best. If these are inordinately large for the given sector of your room, then you could include a well-positioned and well-proportioned amethyst or rose quartz instead. Both of these have the quality of absorbing stale chi and need to be washed under running water prior to their use and thereafter at least every two weeks. To discharge the heavier energy that they gather, place them in the fresh air in the sunlight at least once a fortnight.

Check this sector carefully for signs of instability within any piece of furniture. Pay close attention in particular to your chair and your bed. Unstable support in these sectors will undoubtedly be mirrored in this particular sector of your life.

Wind Chimes

Both hollow, wooden or metal wind chimes form a part of the feng shui toolkit. When it comes to enhancement however, I would recommend using hollow metal wind chimes placed in the sector represented by Metal, which is West or North-west. Water is also supported by Metal and so the North sector is also appropriate. Before purchasing any kind of wind chimes, do make sure that you like the sound of them. Will the other occupants of your home and your neighbours also approve? Always hang them high enough so that you are not consciously aware of them every time you enter the room or sit in that particular sector. Do also remember to select wind chimes that are appropriate in size for the job that you wish to undertake – neither too big nor too small.

Colour

All colours are manifestations of light and chi energy and used appropriately they can be brilliant enhancing tools, uplifting the energy in any room or sector. Refer to the section on the pa kua on pages 25 to 31 to see the appropriate colours to incorporate in the particular sector or room of your home that you wish to develop. Colour associations are not just limited to the world of feng shui. Interior designers are well aware of the properties of colour for enhancing our moods. Colour therapists can recommend the colours of clothing that you wear that best represent your chi in any given situation. A soccer team's kit colours can also represent their chi. England wore red shirts when they won the World Cup final in 1966 – fame!

Chi Stimulation

Look very objectively and carefully for sectors of your home where the chi is potentially blocked. This is often caused by a lack of light or air or if a portion of space is 'missing'. It is easy to redress the imbalance of a poorly lit environment but breaking up stagnant chi in the atmosphere requires more subtle movement or vibration, for example by the use of mobiles, bells or electric fans. Modern household devices including your television set, video, stereo system and radio, can also do the job very well. All of these devices will attract dust so do make the effort to clean this particular area regularly.

Obviously we call in professional architects, interior designers and builders for the difficult jobs, as only a few of us would attempt to rewire or replumb our own homes. However, we all love and need to personalise our homes. Many of the general principles of feng shui are merely common sense and can be applied to many aspects of our homes such as lighting, decor, furniture layout and kitchen design.

Imagery in the form of artwork on the walls can also help stimulate and uplift your chi. Pictures depicting movement, excitement and sunshine have the subconscious effect of uplifting our chi when we look in that direction. A multi-faceted cut-quartz crystal hung in the window just above your eyeline will help to bring available light into the room to brighten it up and stimulate the chi, provided that sector of the room is not full of clutter.

If a section of a room or part of the house is 'missing', there are useful things that you could do to improve that area. Firstly, consider how you need to stimulate the sector that is 'outside' of your home. Rather than let this area accumulate debris and clutter, see it as a valuable place that should be stimulated. This can be done with external lighting at night or by activating the area by bringing some 'life' into it, for example turning it into an area where you gather socially, or placing a bird-table or bird-feeder to attract the light, uplifting chi of wild birds in this sector. Inside of your home you could use mirrors on the two walls of the 'missing' sector to give the impression of depth. Strategically placed, these not only open up the space but also convey the sense of depth and unity. Mirrors are often used in restaurants and hotel lobbies to give that extra feeling of space. Look around a Chinese restaurant to see if it has placed mirrors in the dining room to give the illusion of double the customers, or have they placed one close to the cash register to imply a doubling of income?

Chi Stabilisers

Chi, rather like air, has the capacity at one extreme to stagnate or behave like a hurricane. The purpose of stabilising tools is to slow down, distract or even block the destabilising effects of chi rushing through your home.

Imagine a scenario where you open your front door and you can see all the way through the back door. Chi is going to come gushing in through the front door and escape just as quickly through the back door, taking with it opportunities and leaving eddies of stagnant chi in the adjoining rooms, which are technically going to become backwaters. In this instance, you could use wind chimes or try hanging plants in pots or baskets high enough to avoid a collision with you or your guests. Round, ground level plant pots strategically placed through this corridor can also help slow down the swift movement of chi through your home. By placing them on alternate sides of the corridor, you are in effect creating a meandering course for the chi. Somewhere along this corridor or even at the back door, try hanging a bead curtain.

If you are looking for stability in your life (for example, with relationships) then check that relevant sector for symbolism of stability. Is your relationship a little rocky at present, do you feel it has a future and are you looking for stability? Then, check the South-west sector for any signs of instability – rickety chairs or beds – and think about introducing a feature that speaks of stability, such as any kind of heavy object, figurine, bronze or statue.

Feng shui can incorporate modern and traditional tools to help protect, enhance, stimulate or stabilise various sectors of your home. You have to not only take into account the relevant site and the necessary intention behind its position, but also allow a degree of flexibility which frees your intuition and your taste to apply the final touches. If you absolutely cannot live with the idea of having a crystal in your window or wind chimes in your hallway, then it is important to find something else within the toolkit you are happy with. If, every time you walk past the wind chimes you knock your head and they begin to irritate you, then its effect is bound to be counter-productive. A massive pair of stone lions in your driveway could easily attract unnecessary attention and cause you needless aggravation from your neighbours or local council.

5

A Step-by-Step
Guide To Your Home

Basic feng shui principles can be applied to whatever space
you occupy – a detached home, a terraced house, a flat or
just a room within a shared property. Every home, every
room, every piece of furniture is bound to be unique and you
need to be aware that the conclusions that you draw from
close inspection are not driven by any kind of dogma. Look
out for the glaringly obvious and see what you can do to
practically alter the situation without moving house or calling
in the builders. While you take a tour of your space, note all
the features that you feel need adjusting and later on ratio
nalise these to what is practical and the most necessary at
present. Also make a list of all those small, overlooked
details that you know need fixing at some point – dripping
taps, broken light bulbs, squeaky doors, cracked window
panes, blocked drains, cobwebs and clutter. On a subconscious level, things that need fixing in your home begin to
irritate you and have the potential to block your progress.
When the light bulb goes in your fridge, you immediately
notice it and then very soon, if it is not replaced, the task gets
put on the back burner. However, every time you open the

fridge, you are subconsciously reminded of it and the situation does not support a feeling of harmony and relaxation within you.

To assess or diagnose your home really well, you need to be as objective as possible. This means that you need as much polarity with your space when you do the job. It is for this reason that it is so simple and seemingly intuitive to assess someone else's space when you enter it for the first time. You can immediately sense areas of uplifting chi, stagnation, strange smells. However, you are so used to your own space that it is more of a challenge to see objectively what is going on. I would suggest that, to get the most from this exercise, you leave your home and take a walk round the block. As you do so, look at other properties and begin to notice evidence of cutting chi, blocked driveways, or straight or curving paths. Then when you return to your own property, you have a greater chance of seeing it objectively and relative to adjoining homes in your street.

Paths and Driveways

The 'gateway' into your home is undoubtedly the most important sector to focus on initially, and protecting this area from poison arrows is your first task (see page 13). Ideally, paths and driveways need to be kept clean and clear of any obstacles such as dustbins, bicycles and rubbish. Direct paths from the gate might be helpful for the postman to your front door but chi energy will come to you too fast or violently. Gently curving pathways and drives are ideal. If this is not possible, try to slow down the flow of chi by placing circular plant pots on both its sides to help the chi 'meander' towards the front door. Odd numbers of planters or shrubs are deemed more beneficial. Make sure that plants either side of the path are healthy, as sick or dead plants can affect the health of elderly inhabitants of your home.

Keeping your front garden aesthetically pleasing and tidy will also catch peoples' eyes. With a glance over the fence, they will feel uplifted by the view. On the other hand, if you have a rusting car in your driveway or a broken fence or an old skip, then a passer-by will think negatively and much of this energy will be aimed in your direction.

If your home entrance way leads directly into the street without any driveway or path, then make sure that your doorstep is higher than pavement level. Maintain the doorstep well and keep it clear and clean at all times.

Doors

If your front door is the gateway for chi to enter your home, it is the mouth of your home. Sometimes we consider that we have two front doors, one designed originally by the architect, and another side door or kitchen door we prefer to use more regularly. I would consider the front door to be the one the architect or builder designed and built. Having two front doors can often cause unnecessary arguing and bickering and dithering amongst the occupants.

Make sure that the name of your house or the number is clearly visible for all to see. Is it well lit in the evening? The clearer the identification, the better it is for your career, for your recognition and for ensuring an active social life. When guests visit, it would be the perfect introduction if, on all levels, they felt uplifted by entering your home. On a subconscious level, even how you position the number of your house can have a subtle effect. For example, if the number of your house is 22, then consider positioning the second 2 slightly higher than the first, giving an 'uplifting quality' as it is read.

For real support and protection, your front door needs to be solid. Glass panelling above the door or in its higher sections are fine except in situations where sha chi (poison arrows) is being aimed at your front door. Front doors need to open inwards, allowing beneficial chi to enter your home. The front door also needs to be larger than the back door, encouraging chi to enter through this aspect, and it also needs to be proportional to the size of your home. If it is too big, you could lose opportunities and if it is too small, then the occupants are likely to argue and bicker. If a front door is made up of two panel sections, then they need to be identical in colour and design. Irregularities can lead to confusion and arguments among the inhabitants.

Keep the door clean and freshly painted and regularly oil the hinges and locks. Imagine opening your front door for someone if it squeaks like the door on Dracula's castle. Deep down, it doesn't give your visitor a welcoming feeling! Make sure that your doorbell is easy to locate and that it works. I've often been surprised on consultations how frequently doorbells do not work and that helpful little 'Post-its' even suggest that you need to bang loudly!

On one occasion I visited a young man who had recently moved into a top-floor flat in a modern block. The reason for his feng shui consultation was that he felt out of communication with his friends and his girlfriend since moving to the property. His social life was stagnating and he wondered how it could be reflected within his space. When I got to the block, I could find no doorbell for his apartment. However, on the dot of 3pm. he appeared at the door and welcomed me in. I asked him how people got in touch with him when they visited him and he said he always had a prearranged time and he would then meet them at the main door. It seemed obvious to me that the first thing he could do would be to install a doorbell to open up contact with the outside world!

We all bring dust, dirt and dead chi on our feet into the house. The Japanese are particularly fastidious about leaving shoes at the front door. Worshippers at mosques and temples are also invited to do the same. Culturally, Westerners do not have the same outlook, though at least we usually provide a doormat which is hopefully used by our visitors. Do remember to clean this frequently and replace it annually, as it absorbs dirt and dust and stagnant chi. I spent many years travelling through Third World countries and inevitably, wherever I was, in the early hours around dawn there would be feverish activity in the yard, cleaning and dusting and washing – especially around the main entrance area. In the wealthier, leafier suburbs of England, cleaning the front door and polishing the brass fitments is all part of the daily chore, and in the industrial working heartlands of Britain mothers washed and polished the front step as an almost daily ritual. The whole exercise of keeping this area fresh and bright, opening it to the world while enjoying gossip or communication, helps freshen the home. Living alone and rarely opening the front door creates more of an atmosphere of stagnation and often leads to a life of isolation.

Hallways

Whether this is the hallway of your own home, or one that you share with another tenant, or the lobby in your block of flats, the same fundamental principles apply. Ideally this space needs to be open and well lit. As you enter the hallway, it needs to reveal to the visitor where they are and where they should go next. The more clear this is, the more clear and positive the charge of chi that enters the home.

As you enter some homes, you are often greeted by a

blank wall. This is not ideal, but there are a couple of things that can enhance the situation. An uplifting piece of artwork directly in front of you is helpful, as is laying down a rug or carpet that leads the visitor in the direction they should go. A mirror in this tight corner can be helpful to open up the space, but it should not be placed directly in line with the front door as this will reflect back all the positive chi that is entering.

If, as you enter the home through the front door, you are greeted by an interior door in the hallway, make sure that it hinges in the same way. This is vital, otherwise it can result in confused chi entering the house leading to different levels of 'chaos and confusion' among the occupants. It is preferable to have this second interior door paned with glass, which is more revealing and comforting to the visitor. Another solid door has the potential to block chi too much.

Hallways must be clutter-free zones. Picking your way through walking boots, walking sticks, umbrellas, children's toys and bicycles really does hinder 'opportunity' entering your home. A hallway that leads directly to a toilet is regarded as one of the big feng shui 'no-nos'. The flushing-away process is symbolic of losing money – remember that water is always symbolically associated with cash flow and money. There are no simple solutions to this problem. However the least you can do is keep the door firmly closed at all times.

If, when standing at the front door and looking along the hallway, you can see the back door, then there is another potential problem. Chi will inevitably enter the house and, like a draught, exit through the back door. You really need to look at how to slow down this chi before you are the victim of too many lost opportunities in your life or career. Depending on the length of the hallway through to the back door, you could position two or three wind chimes high enough up to avoid banging your head. You could also place a bead curtain at the back door. If you dislike wind chimes, consider placing hanging baskets. If the top section of the back door is panelled with glass, you may hang a flat piece of red or gold lead-surrounded, glass artwork there to help slow down the lost chi. Ultimately, place plant pots in the hallway to help the chi meander rather than rush through your home.

Corridors

Long, low-ceilinged, dark corridors can be a little bit spooky. This kind of design is often found in schools, hospitals and prisons. Within an apartment block, they are likely to be the source of chi that enters directly into your flat. Ideally, corridors should be bright and airy and any artwork should leave you feeling uplifted. These are certainly not places within our home to hang jaded black and white prints of our long-lost ancestors. These are better repositioned in smaller numbers in the North-west sector of a room (helpful friends) to maintain their continued support and guidance.

The biggest problem with corridors is how to position doors along them. The best situation is to have doorways lined up directly opposite each other along the corridor. The second best situation is to have a doorway with a blank wall opposite. The worst situation is to have one door partially lined up with the door opposite. This lack of harmony between the two doorways will lead to disharmony between the occupants of the rooms, whether this is a situation where a couple of brothers have rooms opposite each other, or whether it involves two neighbours in an apartment block.

Unless a remedy is placed, the occupants are likely to argue and bicker frequently. The solution is to place a mirror on one side of the door facing the door opposite and vice versa. This then creates the impression that the doorways are lined up and opens up the space at the same time.

Windows

From a feng shui perspective, windows are the 'eyes' of the home. They need to be large enough to allow adequate amounts of light and chi to infuse your environment. If they are too small they could leave you feeling like a recluse. Too many windows relative to the size of your space are likely to make you feel too active and can serve as a bigger problem with children, making them hyperactive. Reducing the chi charge through the window can be achieved by installing blinds, either roller blinds or ideally wooden blinds. Windows are best if they are opened outwards and kept spotlessly clean. All cracked panes should be replaced.

Skylights are useful for bringing in extra light, but they are best avoided in some situations. Placing your skylight over the cooker is a big feng shui 'no-no'– this is symbolic of losing your chi and the essence of your food out through the roof. Skylights are otherwise fine in the kitchen, provided they are located away from the cooker. Another poor situation for a skylight is over your bed, as it will allow chi to be dispersed. Definitely avoid this over the bed of a small child, as it can leave them feeling tired and drained and subconsciously it can make them feel uncomfortable as they lack complete privacy and may feel that they are being watched.

Doorways

Internal doors within your home act as smaller 'mouths' or entrances for chi to enter the space. As you enter rooms in many British Victorian homes, doors frequently open on to blank walls in order to give the occupants maximum privacy. To overcome potential problems, either rehang the door to give you full access to the layout of the room as you enter, or hang a full-length mirror on the blank wall that you open on to as a means of opening up the space and giving the occupant of the room a greater feeling of security as they can see who is entering. (Double-check the appropriateness of this second cure when it comes to dealing with your bedroom so that you cannot see yourself in this mirror when you are in bed, as the mirror could drain your chi when you are asleep).

Stairways

In the same way that stairs give us access to different levels of the home, they provide a channel for chi to move freely within your space. In traditional feng shui, an odd number of stairs was always considered to be auspicious. Stairs are best if they are solid rather than slatted, as openings at the back of each step allow the chi to escape and prevent it from easily rising upwards. Ultimately they confuse the chi. In the same way, spiral staircases are regarded as a feng shui no-no as they dissipate and confuse the chi as it tries to rise or fall in the stairwell.

Curving stairways are regarded as the most auspicious but a landing halfway up can also serve the purpose of sedating the chi as it rises or falls. The worst scenario of all is where a front door leads directly to a staircase. This is common in many modern and Victorian homes and leads not only to the loss of opportunity but also to the occupants of the home always being in a rush, coming and going and seldom feeling settled. In many ways this is reinforced by our modern lifestyles where we are always on the move, our work is generally away from home and our daily lives are far from sedentary. One solution to help slow down this rush of chi towards the door from the staircase would be to hang windchimes on the ceiling above the lowest upright support for the banister at the base of the stairs. A heavy statue or figurine at floor level at the base of the stairs could also act to bring stability to the situation. As chi, rather like dust, likes to stagnate in nooks and crannies, keep the stairway freshly brushed and well lit.

Architecturally and aesthetically split-level homes can initially seem pleasing. Rather like Japanese gardens, new vistas are found around every corner. The different levels – such as a drop down into the kitchen, or a slight rise to the dining room – give the home a sense of proportion. However, from a feng shui point of view, they are not regarded as ideal. Chi, rather like water, likes to find its own level. Living on so many levels is likely to cause separation and isolation amongst the inhabitants, so that everyone in the family 'does their own thing', for example, rather than gathering at mealtimes, individual members of the family may eat separately, or watch television, or sit in their room.

Main Bedroom

In feng shui terms, your front door, your bedroom and the position of your cooker are the three most important considerations. We spend between a quarter and a third of our lives in the bedroom, recharging our batteries in an environment that needs to be safe, secure and intimate. Family rooms, kitchens and playrooms are active spaces – yang – whereas the place where we sleep needs to be fundamentally more yin and relaxing. The best position for the main bedroom is furthest away from the front door, preferably diagonally opposite the entrance. On a subliminal level, this gives you the extra feeling of protection, stability and security. The worst possible scenario is to have your bedroom facing or close to the front door.

To set the tone for a harmonious relationship, an equal-sided room with no sectors missing is best. If you have an adjacent toilet or bathroom, always make sure that this doorway is closed when you are asleep. A bedroom positioned above a garage is regarded as a feng shui 'no-no' as the dead space below gives the bedroom a lack of support.

How you decorate and furnish your bedroom is purely personal but there are a few considerations regarding colour from a feng shui point of view. Green has a very calming effect, and while blue is relaxing it can be a little too cool. The colour yellow is very stimulating for the mind so you may become too restless or spend hours and hours at night reading. Peach-coloured walls and furnishings are said to encourage affairs. All shades of red, including pink and salmon encourage romance. Too much red will bring too much fire (yang) into the space, though small amounts in the form of red or pink lampshades, rugs, photo frames or candles can be used to bring the fire of passion into your life.

The most significant feature of the bedroom is the bed itself. Importantly, consider the position of the bed relative to the door. Avoid a situation where the door opens directly on to your bed or where you sleep, directly opposite to the door. Try to position your bed as far from the door as possible but at the same time you should have a good view of it from where you sleep. To bring stability into your relationship, make sure that the bed itself is stable. Make sure that it has a good strong headboard to protect your chi while you are asleep, and avoid sleeping with your head facing an open window else this will drain away your chi. Sleeping directly on the floor is not ideal as it does not allow chi to circulate below you. The gap between your mattress and the floor needs to be kept clear — this is definitely a clutter-free zone! Handy though they may be, storage units under your bed are less than ideal. They have the potential to disturb your sleep and limit the way in which yin (Earth force) recharges you while you sleep.

Double-check the age and quality of your mattress or futon. Did you purchase it new? Did you buy it in a jumble sale? Did someone die in it? Did it belong to your ex-partner? Mattresses have the habit of absorbing chi and need to be turned regularly and given a good few hours in the sunshine every few months. If your mattress or futon is old or second-hand, get rid of it now!

Lying on top of your bed, look up to see what might be raining down on you from above. Avoid sleeping under shelves heavily laden with books and old magazines, or in an alcove with cupboards above your head full of old books. Overhead electrical devices such as lights and fans need to be positioned away from your bed, and a skylight above your bed will allow your chi to dissipate while you sleep. Overhead beams, with their heavy resonance of chi, are likely to cause you restlessness and discomfort as well. They can be made to disappear by painting them the same colour as the ceiling, or by installing a false ceiling. If you live in a wonderful Tudor period house, you might consider having a four-poster bed with a canopy to protect you from the overhead beams.

Mirrors in a bedroom can also be a feng shui nightmare. You should avoid ones that can reflect your image while you are asleep, as this effect can also drain you. Full-length dressing mirrors can be cleverly concealed inside a wardrobe to avoid the problem.

Look around your room for potential sources of disturbing electrical currents from radios, digital clocks, television or personal computers. Ideally, the personal computer should be banished to another part of your home, along with the recharging device for a portable telephone. Radios, clocks, electric radios, clocks and televisions need to be as far as possible away from you while you sleep (read more about electromagnetic pollution on page 121). As with any other room in your home, check the position of your bed for any cutting chi aimed at you from the corners of cupboards, bedside tables, chests of drawners, mantlepieces or fireplaces while you are asleep. Round off any sharp edges and soften them with some kind of cover or drape. Create a relaxing yet warm atmosphere in the bedroom through different forms of lighting. Experiment until you find a solution that is both practical and aesthetically pleasing. A good reading light can also be balanced by the more romantic feel of candlelight as well. Check the South-west sector of your bedroom as this relates to relationships. Avoid putting your dirty linen basket in this section! Current, happy photographs of you and your partner and any kind of symbolism of relationship in this sector is ideal.

On waking up, you can be greatly motivated if you are greeted by a photograph, poster or painting on the wall ahead of you. It needs to be an image that is both tranquil and uplifting and epitomises your journey in life. Think of a special, inspiring landscape. Every morning we wake up to new possibilities – the image in front of you should reflect this while a blank wall or an image of struggle might have detrimental effects.

To really get your day off to a good start, always remember to make your bed! Leaving an unfinished bed and a trail of clothing that didn't make it to the laundry basket can get you off to an incomplete and messy start in the morning.

Kitchen

The layout of the kitchen, in particular the position of your cooker, can bring great benefits to the wealth and health of the family as a whole and is vitally important from a feng shui perspective. This is, after all, the heart (hearth) of your home. This is where we prepare our food, which directly becomes our blood, which in turn fuels, nourishes and invigorates us. Since our health and vitality are so closely linked to what we cook and eat, it is essential that this space is fresh, airy, uplifting and peaceful. The ideal position for the kitchen is far away from the front door, and sheltered from the day-to-day rush of traffic throughout the house. It needs to be a peaceful environment where the cook will feel undisturbed and unthreatened.

Twenty-five years ago I spent six months travelling through the Far East and enjoyed the hospitality of Chinese merchant families on many occasions. Their generosity with food was always enormous. Although so much family life was centred around eating, I was seldom aware of the kitchen and least of all invited to enter the kitchen to browse in their fridge or lift the lids of the pots while the cook was preparing the meal. In Muslim cultures in Africa and the Middle East, I have enjoyed similar hospitality and it is an unwritten rule that you do not go and make yourself at home in their kitchen. Traditionally, this is a vital and sacred space that brings harmony and health to all the family and their guests.

In our busy and high-tech world, the kitchen has been relegated to nothing more than a large larder in many new home designs. The size and layout of the kitchen really mirrors the contemporary view that preparing and cooking food is a chore. Time is the most important commodity in our lives at present. On the other hand the kitchen has also become a focal point in modern life. Apart from cooking and laundering facilities, it often incorporates our dining area, our communication network (telephone) and even televisions and radios. Whatever situation works best for you regarding your lifestyle or the layout of your home, fundamental feng shui principles can be applied.

Regarding clutter, as described on page 62, make sure that this space is kept immaculately clean. Go through all the cupboards and drawers and get rid of old or dead food, out-of-date packages and seldom-used crockery. Keep the fridge clean and well stocked.

An abundance in your cupboards, larder and fridge mirrors the abundance in your life. Cooking a little more than you need does not necessarily create a situation of waste or a temptation to overeat. It can also encourage more guests to arrive. Being more generous as a host encourages a more active social life at the same time.

Naturally, your cooker is associated with the Element Fire. This Element is a microcosm of the sun. Without it, life would not exist. In our evolution we became civilised when we began to harness its energy and its discovery had parallel developments in terms of our ability to communicate, cultivate and make tools. Our whole modern civilisation is built around the Element Fire — manufacturing, electricity, communications and so forth. We also have the potential to destroy ourselves a hundredfold through atomic warfare and other weapons of mass destruction. Fire, if harnessed wisely, can bring us good health and prosperity, whereas handled poorly, it can have a very destructive nature. Bringing Fire into our home and into our cooking is essential if we are living in a cold, damp, cloudy environment.

Bringing the best quality of the Fire into your home would translate on a practical level to the use of a gas cooker rather than an electric or microwave device. On a chemical level, cooking with electric or microwave energy does not affect the composition of the food but it lacks the chi of real fire.

Never have your back to the door while you are working at the cooker. This creates a sense of insecurity as you cannot see who is approaching from behind. If your cooker is already positioned like this, then you could consider placing mirrors behind or adjacent to the stove to give you a view of the door behind you. Try to avoid placing the cooker in a tight corner. The circulation of chi is always poorer in recesses and corners, as you will know from moving furniture when spring-cleaning. Never stand under a beam when you are cooking as this can leave you feeling under pressure while you prepare the food. Make sure that everything about your cooking appliance is functional. Is it easy to use, is it easy to keep clean? Avoid placing the cooker directly below the skylight as this allows beneficial chi to escape upwards. And make sure that the oven door does not open with a direct view either towards the front door, a toilet, or a bedroom.

Extractor fans and hoods are often a necessity in modern, less ventilated kitchens. Try to choose one that is as quiet as possible as, on a subliminal level, their noise is irritating and disturbs your concentration. Make sure that they are sufficiently built-in and recessed so as not to create cutting chi which can rain down on your head while you are standing at the stove. Massive stainless steel or copper hoods may look aesthetically pleasing but they create an almost knife-like edge of cutting chi.

You should pay special attention to Fire and Water, the two elements represented by the cooker and the sink. The fridge or freezer also belongs to Water Element. They are fundamental necessities in any kitchen yet their intrinsic nature creates opposition. Water puts out Fire and Fire creates steam with Water. Be careful not to place these two Elements in opposition to each other on opposite sides of the work space or sitting adjacent to each other. In many kitchens it is impractical to change this so as a remedy you might consider introducing the Element that is the buffer between Fire and Water – Wood, or one of its colours, green or blue. Try hanging your wooden bread-board between the fridge and the cooker. Install green or blue reflective tiles on the splashback between the cooker and the sink if they are adjacent, or place a wooden stool or table in the space between the cooker and sink if they are on opposite sides of the room.

It is vital to foster harmony in the kitchen. Years ago I went to teach cooking in a wealthy client's kitchen. It was a feng shui nightmare. All my preconceived plans about what I was going to demonstrate flew out of the window in an instant as the distractions in the kitchen were overwhelming. The television was going full blast even though my client wasn't watching it, the telephone interrupted us every few minutes, a large dog was languishing on the floor just in front of the sink, two cats came and went as they pleased through the cat-flap and a rather fine mynah bird vented its feelings all morning long! In addition to these distractions, a maid was busy at the other end of the kitchen doing the laundry.

In reality, kitchens are, for many of us, the focus of our

lives. Do, however, minimise the use of the television or the telephone while you are cooking. If you are also using the kitchen as a place to eat, then try to demarcate that particular area by creating a separate 'island' for it. You could choose to carpet the dining area and tile the kitchen preparation area. You may want to use different cabinets and furniture in the dining section. The chi of relaxing while you eat is essentially different from the chi we need when we are preparing our food. It is a subtle task of integrating the cook with the dining area without overprotecting them so that they feel completely isolated and out of touch with the rest of the family.

Greens and yellows are very good colours in the kitchen and any kind of real wood or laminate wood effect can be beneficial (Wood supports Fire). As you take a closer look at your kitchen, look out for any sources of cutting chi emanating from the sharp edges of dressers, cupboards, sideboards and tables and aimed at the cook or people relaxing at the dining table.

Dining Room, Dining Area

Most of the principles that apply to a good feng shui layout for your dining room apply equally to a corner of your kitchen or lounge designated for eating. Ideally, the dining room lies away from the noise and distractions of the rest of the house and the hustle and bustle of the road outside. Two of the main aims in designing the dining area need to be the creation of a relaxing atmosphere to aid digestion, and the formation of a comfortable seating arrangement that allows for good communication around the table.

I am convinced that fast food restaurants have employed some of these feng shui principles for purely the opposite effect. The lighting and the decor is loud and garish and the seating stark and uncomfortable, and they simply encourage you to eat and move on as fast as possible – all the better for turnover!

To create a relaxing atmosphere within the dining area, choose colours that encourage a more mellow feeling. Various shades of green are ideal, and yellows are very good at stimulating the mind, making for lively discussions and debates around the table. Create different effects with lighting and this is especially important if this area is part of your lounge or kitchen. Keeping the area that you eat out of the main thoroughfare in the kitchen and the lounge is best, as this constant movement of chi distracts those that are eating.

For real comfort and communication at mealtimes, look no further than the furniture that you will be using – the table and chairs. A solid wooden table set in the centre of the room is far more likely to encourage stability and communication than a narrow breakfast bar arrangement, where diners sit precariously on stools without real support for their backs. Round or octagonal-shaped tables are ideal as everyone is equally positioned around the table. Oval and rectangular tables can create a sense of hierarchy as at least two people are going to dominate the table by their positions at either end. Chairs need to be really comfortable and have support reaching up at least as high as the shoulders. Chairs with elbow supports tend to create division and segregation around the table.

Works of art and photographs are fine in the dining area, provided they do not have an overbearing presence and distract guests from their meal. Ideally you need to focus their attention on the table. A large mirror on the wall adjacent to the dining table creates the effect of doubling up the quantities being served. This is good feng shui as it encourages a feeling of prosperity and success. If you do have a separate dining room then leave the door open when the room is not in use, as this encourages chi to enter the room and invites prosperity. Do check the position of every chair to ensure that no one is sitting under a beam or has cutting chi aimed at them from nearby furniture, mantlepieces or other structures.

If you have a serving hatch through to the kitchen, be sure to close this while you are eating so that guests do not feel distracted by busy activity in the kitchen. If your dining area is a section of your lounge or kitchen, then, in addition to creating a different atmosphere within this space, try incorporating a lightweight screen to shield the cook and, at the same time, prevent the cook's activity from distracting the ambience that you have created.

Lounge, Family Room

Your lounge is the centrepiece of your home, the place where you and your family are on show. While being both welcoming and comfortable, it can maintain a gentle, formal atmosphere. The layout of the room, the items you have on display and the ambience the room creates come together to act as a metaphor for your life and your success. A family room, on the other hand, can be relaxing, fun, informal, and even a little untidy. Furniture can be mobile to allow greater flexibility for the occupants. Provided the family room is used on a daily basis, there is little likelihood of clutter accumulating in a negative way.

The main function of the traditional family lounge was communication and its main feature was the fireplace; sofas and chairs were arranged to benefit from its warmth. This focal point has been replaced nowadays by the television and most furniture is lined up to benefit from the best view. This has the potential to lessen communication between family members. A practical solution would be to create a new focus for attention in the room. Having two sofas facing each other in a central aspect of the room with a coffee table in between can create a new focus for people's attention.

On a practical level, try to site the seating area away from any 'draughts' of chi. Check whether there is a window directly opposite the door when you enter the room, as you and your guests would be uncomfortable sitting directly in this 'draught'. For maximum comfort within the lounge, avoid seating yourself or guests with your backs to the door. Avoid positioning sofas underneath beams or very bright lights. Storage cabinets, coffee tables or occasional tables are best if they have rounded edges to avoid cutting chi but they can be covered with drapes to soften the effect. Sofas and armchairs are perfect when they have plenty of support behind them (the Turtle) and if you choose a layout where two sofas face each other note that too much distance can cause excess formality while if they are too close too much intimacy can be created.

The lounge is a wonderful space and you can bring sparkle to its every sector. Pay special attention to the South-west sector, relating to relationships, and the South-east sector, relating to wealth and blessings. Don't make the mistake of over-stimulating these two sectors and avoiding the sectors diametrically opposite them representing contemplation and helpful friends.

Finally, wander around the lounge and feel how easy it is to circulate within the room. Can you move around freely without tripping over too much furniture? If you find it difficult so will your guests and at the same time chi is more likely to stagnate within the space.

Children's Bedroom

The most obvious factors to take into consideration regarding the children's bedroom is that they are growing, exploring, curious, active, unique and evolving into their true potential. How can you begin to create a space which can reflect all these needs? Given that they spend a third of their formative life in this space, it is vital that the bedroom reflects their personality and desire to grow and explore. Green and blue decor has a relaxing effect, while shades of yellow can stimulate their mind (though be sure yellow is not particularly bright as it might cause insomnia).

Try to keep the central sector of the bedroom floor free for them to use as they please. Whether this is for games, projects or simply wrestling with their siblings or friends, it needs to be open and free for the circulation of chi. Generally speaking, mobiles are excellent in children's bedrooms. They help to circulate the chi within the space, though I would not recommend placing them directly over their head while they are asleep. The position of their bed relative to the door is also vital, as with adults. However, do let them experiment with where they feel most comfortable sleeping within the room.

For younger children, it is important that furniture brought into the room is of the same scale as them. Living in an adult world they may feel that they are in Lilliput, surrounded by massive people, huge furniture and wardrobes that look or feel the size of houses. Position a full-length mirror from the floor upwards so that they can see themselves, though avoid placing this where their image is reflected while they are asleep. Allow older children the freedom to personalise their space, letting them choose colours, wallpaper and layout. It is one thing to consider what we think is appropriate, but they inevitably have a very different idea.

If two children share the same bedroom, then try to create some form of screen to allow them to personalise and individualise their own sector of the room. Children, like adults, need their own space. Make sure that they have good access to controlling the lighting of the room, and that any bedside light is quick and easy for them to find.

Sleeping under skylights, beams and shelves laden with books and puzzles is certainly not ideal. The pressure from above can give them headaches and disturb their night's rest. Children adore bunk beds – they are an adventure and they have a choice between sleeping on top and sleeping underneath – and fighting for their preference! If this is the only solution in the available space, make sure that the children change their bunk regularly. Sleeping on the lower bunk gives a feeling of being under pressure, being in a cave, whereas sleeping on the top can leave them feeling worried about falling off. To soften this effect, consider painting the 'ceiling' created by the upper bunk a light colour to give more of an impression of space for the child on the lower bunk.

Bedroom for the Elderly

There are various practical feng shui considerations regarding the creation of a 'haven' for elderly residents or guests of your home. Throughout the Third World, it is not unusual for grandparents to continue living as part of a family unit in which they play a vital role. Whatever culture they come from, they all need one thing – a sense of security, which can present itself as freedom from worries about their health, or the absence of any threat of violence. In considering what can support an elderly person within your home, it is important to bring a sense of security and independence into this space.

Traditional feng shui wisdom always suggests that elderly people are more comfortable occupying the West sector of the home, avoiding the harsh early sunlight while enjoying the more mellow western half of the home which reflects their position in their journey in life. It is best to locate their room away from the busy areas of the home so that they can enjoy their quiet, their space and their independence. Ideally, toilet or bathroom should be handy so that they do not have to wander up and downstairs during the night. Mellow colours including off-whites, salmon or beige colours, are ideal for the decor. They should be encouraged to keep plenty of fresh plants, rather than dried flowers, as well as a large display of current photographs of their family and friends rather than a selection of family photographs from the past.

Study, Work Station

This room or section of a room needs careful consideration. To begin with, it is important that you define the primary purpose of this space. Is it an area designated for your children to get on with their homework? Is it simply a desk where you keep up to date with your correspondence and bills? Is this where you bring work home and spend several hours in the evenings or weekends completing projects? Is this an area where you study for a course of diploma? All of these uses need stabilisation, focus, stillness and peace.

On the other hand you may be working from home. A large proportion of your time needs to be engaged in communication with the outside world. If you become isolated and lack the charge of the interaction with colleagues and clients, it could easily lead to you being sidelined and forgotten. In this particular instance, you need to be looking at ways to vitalise this area and increase the potential for you to communicate with the outside world.

Whatever your desired use for this space, basic feng shui considerations can be applied. Ideally this area is quiet, without distractions, and is out of the main thoroughfare of the home. The position and structure of both your desk and chair are vital. A common mistake is to place a desk up against a wall with layer of layer of useful shelves towering above, heavily laden with books and notes and magazines. This is a feng shui nightmare! From this perspective you are likely to feel trapped, overburdened and uninspired. Just to complete the nightmare, have your back facing the door!

The first step is to make sure that you have a desk that is strong, stable and clutter free, both on the surface and within the drawers. The imagery of study and contemplation is represented by Ken, the Mountain trigram from the *I Ching*. Your desk ideally represents this image. Secondly, make sure that the chair you use is stable and gives your back good support. It is fine if the chair swivels and you can adjust its height and angle, but it must have a good 'mountain' behind. Get these two pieces of furniture firmly stable and you will bring stability to your studies of work.

The next job is to look at the position of your desk and chair relative to the room. In an ideal world, we would position ourselves in the sector of study and contemplation, which is in the North-east. Even if you do not position yourself in this sector in your study, make sure that the South-east corner is kept clutter-free, bright and inspiring. Try to position yourself so that you can see the door from where you sit, and avoid a situation where you could be placed in the 'draught' of chi that could occur if there is a window opposite the door. Similarly, check that you are not positioning yourself in a through draught of chi that may be occurring if you sit midway or along the path or in the direct line of two facing windows. This will affect your concentration, as your ideas will leave via the window!

Daylight from the windows can be very uplifting and inspiring but try to avoid positioning your desk so that you are looking directly out of the window. You may find yourself being constantly distracted. Sitting close enough to benefit from the sunlight and at a glance being able to see the view sideways is far better than looking directly out of the window or being stuck in some dimly lit corner. Images of stability, such as mountainous landscapes, can help you focus, while images of moving water such as lakes, streams and oceans can help bring you inspiration.

If, when working from home, it is vital for you to communicate with clients and colleagues in the outside world then there are various ways in which you can keep in contact. Initially, you must deal with the obvious. Keep your desk a clutter-free zone and deal with any outstanding bills, memos, enquiries and commitments, as until these are really effectively finished with you are blocking the potential for new possibilities to arrive. Pay particular attention next to the North-West sector of your study, representing mentor, helpful friends and potential for international trade and travel. Obviously keep this area clutter free and consider positioning your communications system within this sector — your telephone or fax machine. Keep the area well lit, bring in some sparkle and, if you wish to open up contact and communication with all four corners of the world, consider placing an illuminated globe in this sector.

If this room is also going to be used for your lounge or dining area, then remember that both of these activities are yin and relaxing compared to the yang activity of the communication and focus required by your work. Make the effort to discipline your time when you designate this a yang area during office hours, and then look at how you can simply transform the space by the use of screens or colours to create a more relaxing atmosphere for meal times, socialising or watching television.

Bathroom, Toilet

There are two important considerations about the location and use of this space. Firstly, the bathroom and toilet are primarily governed by and driven by the Element Water. In feng shui, Water is associated with wealth, prosperity, career and good cash flow. Secondly, the function of these rooms is associated with elimination and waste. With these two considerations in mind, it is easier to demystify the rules applying to the layout and location of this space.

Inauspicious locations for the toilet include:

☆ Opposite the kitchen. The Elements of Fire and Water will clash in this situation. The leap from the preparation of the food (kitchen) to the elimination of food (toilet) is too violent for this to be seen as an auspicious position.

☆ Adjacent to the front door. In feng shui, we can regard the doorway as the mouth of our home, where career and opportunities enter, whereas the toilet is clearly at the other end of this process and needs to be as far away as possible.

☆ Directly opposite the front door, even if this is at the end of a passage. This kind of position can lead to wasted opportunities and lost prospects, both career-wise and financially.

☆ Dead centre. This is the worst location for the toilet in the family home or a business. It is quite a common feature in houses where the builder has considerately installed a toilet under the stairs, but from a feng shui point of view this is considered a disaster for your health and financial prospects. The centre of your home (the tai chi) is best left either open or with some focus for your attention, such as a statue, table or plant. What is not suited in this situation is a space associated with waste and loss. Before you give up in desperation, a possible remedy is to place a full-length mirror on the outside of the toilet door, thus giving the impression that the toilet does not exist.

Always keep the toilet door shut and insist that the occupants of the house keep the lid of the toilet down to suppress any loss of chi and luck.

For both the bathroom and the toilet, always make sure the plumbing fixtures are spotlessly clean and work. Dripping taps encourage you to waste money and noisy plumbing and cisterns are disturbing on a subliminal level. Keep the area light, airy and well lit. Ideal colours for the bathroom or the toilet include light greys, creams and pale blues.

If your toilet is located in the South-east sector of your home, representing wealth and blessings, a full-length mirror placed on the outside of the door may help. To help counteract money and opportunities being flushed away, consider keeping a bowl of pebbles on the shelf above the toilet or on the cistern itself. This concentrated form of Earth energy will help to control water. A black- or red-coloured rug at the base of the pedestal could also be used as a protective device.

The bathroom is often the first place we visit in the morning. When you wash and prepare yourself for the day, you need to have the largest possible view of yourself at that time. I don't recommend tiling your entire bathroom wall with mirrors but do place a large mirror above the wash-basin to help you start the day with a big clear, bright vision. A small, round cracked mirror is going to limit your possibil-ities. Likewise a mirror that is split in two – a very common feature of bathroom cabinets – can also get you off to a difficult start. You are not seeing the whole picture. If a drain sits in a basin or a bath in the South-east sector, keep the plug in when you are not using it to prevent loss of money.

Attic Room, Loft

Opening up this area of your home can be a very useful way of creating additional floor space. Always begin your assess-ment by placing the pa kua over the entire area and be clear of the compass directions and the sectors that are repre-sented. The main feng shui factors to take into consideration are that this space is going to be somewhat isolated from the rest of the house, higher up and more vulnerable to the elements. Living in a loft can have this attraction for people because they are looking for a sense of isolation, simplicity and lightness (yin) that the space can bring. It is important therefore to bring elements of 'stability' into the space, including figurines, statues, earthenware pots and heavy planters for small indoor trees and plants. In Western Europe, attics and lofts have always been designated for storage or for the accommodation of servants, and in recent years, they have also formed the source of cheaper accommo-dation for students, resting actors, budding artists. Being higher up, closer to the heavens, the attic or the loft can be a very inspiring space to live and work – many young poets and artists began their careers in such a space.

The main problems from a feng shui perspective are sloping

ceilings, skylights or beams but there are methods to reduce some of their effects. If you are lucky enough to live in an attic with cathedral-proportioned roofs, you do not need to be too concerned about the direct effect of the skylights upon you. However in most situations a skylight may be only one or two feet above your head. Despite the temptation, it is not wise to either sleep or work directly under one of these as the strength of yang chi descending through the skylight can cause difficulty in sleeping and concentration, especially at night. Try to position your desk or bed slightly to the side of the skylight. To slow down the full force of yang, hang wind chimes at the top of the skylight to disperse some of this chi. Cutting chi from beams, and the extra 'weight' that they bring to the space, can be softened by either covering them or painting them.

The biggest problem with the attic is the inevitable sloping ceiling. Although far from ideal as it does not give you a consistent level of yang chi bearing down on you, you can do little to remedy this other than by creating more dormer windows and alcoves. The hours of sleep, when we recharge ourselves, form the most important part of our day, so you could create a false ceiling by using a drape or canopy above the bed to give the feel of a level ceiling above you.

Basement

This space has a very strong yin charge. Located deep in the foundations of the building, often with thick floors and walls, it is inevitably going to be cooler, darker and perhaps damper. Given these prevailing factors, when you work or live in a basement you should think of ways in which you might need to redress this imbalance.

To bring uplifting energy into the space, it is essential to focus immediately on the lighting. Utilise whatever natural daylight you have within the space and supplement this with full spectrum lighting which is healthy both for you and for any plant life. Use colours and decor that are brighter and lighter, especially the lighter shades of green, blue and yellow. Plants are a great source of yin energy – I highly recommend ferns and peace lilies in this area. Another important source of yin is fresh air, so look at how and where this enters the basement, install adequate ventilation where there is no natural source and keep doors other than those to bathrooms and toilets open to allow the circulation of chi and air.

Pay particular attention to the flooring. Below your feet is probably half a metre of concrete which is cold and yin, and beneath that the soil is equally yin. Make sure there is plenty of good quality, environmentally friendly insulation sand-wiched between the concrete and ideally a wooden floor, which in turn is covered in luxuriant warm carpet. Any signs of condensation or dampness need to be remedied as soon as possible and in the short term you could consider using a dehumidifier.

Finally, to open up any space that is lacking in natural light through the windows, you can open up and expand (yinise) your space with the use of large mirrors.

Since feng shui is essentially about balance and harmony in our own lives and the space that we inhabit, remember that living in a basement leaves you with greater potential for isolation and hibernation. If this is not what you desire, then make sure that your entrance way is clear and well illumi-nated and that your name plate and doorbell are easy to access. Devote more energy than usual to inviting friends round for dinner and to socialising, and at the same time make the effort to spend some of your recreation time in the open.

Garden

If you have a garden, it is well worth looking at it from a feng shui perspective to see if its layout and style reflects what you are trying to achieve within your home. Whether you have a small balcony, a postage stamp front garden, a patio or a large garden, you can still place the pa kua grid over the space to see where all the relevant sectors lie. In the same way that you may have wished to enhance the South-West sector of your room or home (relationships), you can begin to become aware of where this sector lies within your garden and how the current state of it reflects what you are trying to achieve.

In an ideal feng shui world, we would approach the front door by stepping up towards it. A perfect scenario would have a slight gradient, whether a rising pathway or gently curving steps towards the front door. If you have the opposite situation where you walk or approach your front door by coming down a slope, you could remedy this by installing a bright light with an uplighter on either side of the front door. Similarly, the name of your house or the number of your house could have the letters or numbers written so that they rise toward the end of the sign. At the back of the house, following Form School feng shui, it is ideal to have some form of protection. Traditionally we know that this meant a hill or a slope or a mountain behind you. If your garden slopes downwards away from the house at the back, then consider creating some kind of false mountain at the bottom of the garden. A hedge or a fence with a trellis along the top would give you support. Without this mountain behind you, it is possible that your energy and financial resources will be drained.

Just as important in the garden as it was in the house is the need to primarily deal with the rubbish, debris and broken fixtures. Check and see what could really go and what needs fixing. Look out for fences that need repairing, cracks in paving slabs, broken glass in conservatories or greenhouses and broken or squeaky gates.

If you really want to go to town and use feng shui principles to redesign your garden, then I highly recommend Gill Hale's book (see p. 136) for some inspiring ideas. Without necessarily turning your garden into a Zen temple garden overnight, some very practical feng shui principles can be easy applied to your garden space. Consider what you really want from your garden and how much time and money you have to spend on it. The beauty and simplicity of feng shui in the garden is that it is primarily based on principles of yin and yang, which can provide the secret to creating variety. Ideally, therefore, you would have areas of stillness and areas of activity, as well as some areas that are light and open and others that are shaded and hidden. Areas that are landscaped can have features that are higher and lower, and introduce elements of water and rock formations. By bringing many different aspects into the garden, it creates a sense of intrigue and surprise as you meander through the space. Gently curving pathways, clumps of bushes, ponds, waterfalls, fountains, bird-baths, rockeries, barbecue areas, compost heaps, meditation areas and play areas are just some of the focal points that you may wish to build. If you would like to use your garden primarily for entertaining friends, then consider how to develop the South-west sector of the garden (relationships) to best serve that purpose. This really isn't the site for a compost heap or a rotting garden shed.

Your home and your garden are the places where you spend most of the time in what are relatively yin activities – resting, recharging, sleeping, contemplating and eating –

while the traditional yang activities of hunting, farming, working, travelling and selling occur outside of the home. In many ways our home is our castle. When it comes to looking at your garden from this perspective, make sure that you have adequate protection. If your front garden borders on to a busy road, consider planting a hedge or, if space allows, planting trees, preferably in odd numbers three, five, seven, and so on. Trees act as wonderful guardians for your property but they need always to be healthy otherwise they can undermine the health of the occupants, especially the elderly. Protection in the back garden can come from walls, fences, hedges, shrubbery and trellises. In the northern hemisphere, where the prevailing colder elements come from the North and the East, it is wise to plant or place some form of protection to ward off the cold chill. As the colour red is often associated with protection, you could place planters with hardy red geraniums either side of your front door.

Just as you choose colours within different rooms of your home to enhance the effects of either its use or the sector it represents, the selection and colours of flowers in your garden can have a similar effect. Greenery, especially evergreens, give a sense of stamina, strength and determination to see things through. White is the colour of purity in many cultures, and yellow blossoms and flowers help stimulate the intellect, whereas red acts as both a protector for your health and finances as well as being a particularly energising colour. If you have space for a lawn, do not be overly concerned any more about the ubiquitous dandelion. In full flower on your lawn, from a feng shui perspective, they are a sign of luck and affluence, rather than a lazy gardener!

Finally, do consider installing features or growing plants that encourage wildlife into your garden. Bees, butterflies and birds help to activate the chi in much the same way that a clean fresh water feature or a few well-positioned garden lights at night can help produce a similar effect.

Your garden has enormous potential to be transformed using feng shui principles in the same way as the interior of your home – enjoy!

Buying a Home

Here are some useful feng shui pointers if you are on the verge of buying a new home. When assessing the property's suitability in terms of various factors such as location, price and access to work or school, I would allow considerations based on feng shui, to govern 30 per cent of my overall decision.

Firstly, any traditional Form School feng shui expert would check the landscape at all times of day and night in order to notice all subtle changes. On a practical level, this means checking out the neighbourhood from an objective point of view. Mingle in the local pub, visit some of the local shops and visit the location at different times of the day and night. What seemed like a quiet little cul de sac on a Saturday afternoon could turn into the equivalent of Piccadilly Circus on a Monday morning during the rush hour. Next, what are the neighbours like? This is a difficult one to investigate but remember that their chi will inevitably affect you in either a subtle or a dramatic way. Next, what do you know about the current and previous owners? Have they moved on to bigger and better properties and jobs? Have they been made redundant? Check the front door for any signs of poison arrows aimed in its direction. What is the form of the approach to the house – does it offer protection?

Inside the home be particularly wary of some of the bigger

feng shui challenges, such as the front and the rear door being positioned along a straight line. Will this be easy enough to remedy, or would it be simpler to start looking at another property? With your compass check which sector of the home the toilets and bathroom occupy. If they are right at the centre of the house or occupying the South-east sector (wealth and blessings), then you might feel that this is too great a challenge. For your long-term health and prosperity, look closely at the kitchen and pay particular attention to the relationship of Fire and Water. If this is a problem, do you have the budget to redesign the kitchen to suit your needs?

Finally, consider the direction you and your family are moving along in order to relocate to this property. Whether this is 100 yards or 100 miles, which compass direction will it follow? For more insights into this aspect of feng shui, please refer to page 40.

Selling Your Home

When you wish to sell your property, follow the obvious advice that you would get from your estate agent. Namely, keep the home clean and fresh, deal with any unfinished projects and create a warm and inviting atmosphere at all times. These factors help to create an initial impression for potential purchasers when they first visit your property. In the same way that I have encouraged you to deal with all the small repairs within your home, these also need to be taken into account when you sell as, on a subliminal level, they irritate and go against what you are trying to achieve. They have the potential to block progress.

From a feng shui perspective, you need to be very clear in your intention. What are you trying to achieve? In any Oriental discipline, whether it is flower-arranging, martial arts or meditation, you need to have a clear goal and vision to follow with your chi. It is no good dabbling in selling your home. You need to focus all of your chi on achieving your dream, your target and getting your price.

A feng shui 'cure' that has been used by several clients and friends, with amazing effects may be of use. It has helped to speed up the sale process and also to attract the kind of purchaser who is not going to squabble or delay. You need to take a tiny chip of wood from either the floorboard or a skirting board and hold it firmly in your fist. With this piece of your property within your grasp, you need to keep alive your intention to sell the property. You then need to cast this piece of your home into flowing water at the most active time of the day, between 11am and 1pm. Ideally, you have a large river within a few miles where you can deposit this. If it is close by, simply walk there between these hours, continuously thinking about selling, and cast it away. Alternatively, have someone drive you to the river while you concentrate on letting the property go and, again, deposit this chip of your house between those times.

6

The Development of Feng Shui

The applications of feng shui principles in our culture are limitless. Imagine the possibility in the future of designing schools along feng shui lines, taking space vital to the growth of the next generation and considering how best to use it to help students develop awareness and communication skills. Imagine designing hospitals that were essentially healing environments. The layout, lighting, decor and circulation of chi could all be planned to benefit not only the patients but also the healers. Imagine designing prisons that were not dead-ends and dungeons, but created an environment that fostered trust, new possibility, communication and education – it would certainly have an impact on the occupants. Imagine designing offices that really supported the 'human' occupants. Far from feeling drained, tired and unenthusiastic, employees would have a greater chance of feeling motivated and inspired in their workspace. The choice of appropriate lighting and decor and the positioning of key members of staff and departments in the appropriate sectors of the office could all make a difference. Imagine designing housing estates and individual homes around feng shui principles, built into the environment with a sense of community and security and constructed to accommodate basic considerations about the positioning of doors, windows, kitchens and toilets.

So much energy is nowadays devoted to fixing, repairing or curing that which is not working. In an ideal world, more time needs to be spent on the preventing.

The future of feng shui in the West lies in embracing the principles of this system, while at the same time adapting how you manifest and practise feng shui in a way that suits contemporary lives. To negotiate your way around London, you need a contemporary map rather than an ancient map of Peking! By honouring the origins and the principles of the system, we can best move ahead by being flexible and adaptable with its practice. Having been over the years a student of different Oriental specialties, I have always valued the advice I was given by one master. 'Don't doubt the principle but do doubt the practice.' A sound grounding in the principles of any system gives you greater adaptability and flexibility to interpret the practice. Start to doubt, question and alter the principles and you easily lack a foundation for your practice. Traditional acupuncture is even older than feng shui yet there were no remedies or cures in the old textbooks for a modern disease such as ME. However, you would have no difficulty in consulting an acupuncturist for such a problem nowadays. They would not have to look up ME in their manual. They know the principles of diagnosis and treatment and they adapt and develop their treatments according to these age-old standards. The core of acupuncture, as with so many other Eastern healing systems, remains rooted in principles and yet its practice can be widely adapted to different situations.

Ultimately, feng shui is about creating health, prosperity and harmony in our lives. These are all expressions of our freedom. What greater goals could we have than clear self-expression, or vibrant health, or nurturing relationships? What we do not need is to be restricted or tied down by dogma or to become overly neurotic about everything that we do. The creation of environments harmonious with your dream can only benefit you by granting more freedom in your life. By working with the tides and currents of chi in a creative way, it will undoubtedly have a fulfilling effect on your life.

With the growing interest of feng shui in the West, a number of specialist areas have begun to enjoy greater levels of awareness as a result. An understanding of geopathic stress, earth acupuncture and space clearing is intrinsic to traditional feng shui. These systems all have something special to offer which can only enhance and give greater depth to our appreciation of space.

Space Clearing

It is a relatively simple process to change our own chi if it becomes stagnant. Typical symptoms include tiredness, depression, loss of appetite, moodiness or melancholy. A bracing walk, a shower, a refreshing meal or some stimulating and strenuous activity all have the potential to change your chi quite quickly. The chi of a building can take longer to change as it absorbs stagnant energy much more deeply. Concrete, bricks, stone and wood have the capacity to absorb stagnant chi over time and, because of their yang nature, it takes longer to discharge. One of the major factors that is taken into consideration in feng shui is known as the 'predecessor energy', the vibration left behind by the previous owner – a reflection of their health, their moods and their chi. Next time you visit an empty flat or home, notice the pathways ground into the carpet where the previous occupants have walked to and fro. In major rooms and areas it is easy to spot main thoroughfares and the former locations of furniture, as well as corners of the space that have been relatively inactive.

On another level, all of us have experienced walking into a room where two people have just been engaged in an argument. We literally feel the atmosphere could be cut with a knife. Similarly, we are all aware of the energy of staff in a shop or an office when we enter. Sometimes the chi is bubbly, effervescent and enthusiastic and at other times you are greeted by a wall of gloom, despondency, fear or complacency.

Space clearing is a ritual found in almost every traditional or native culture. In the West, it is probably mostly linked to spring-cleaning, a house-warming party to enliven a new home or a blessing from the local priest. It is the skill of changing the atmosphere in the home from one of stagnant chi to one of vibrant, health-promoting and spiritually enhancing chi. Space clearing before moving into a new home was considered a vital part of any move in traditional cultures and it is still practised in some form today throughout the world. Rituals can include the use of herbs, chants, potions, symbolism, spiritual ceremonies, blessings, sacrifices, gifts, fruits, plants, holy water and sometimes timing to coincide with the planets or moon cycles. Space clearing can be drawn from the Native American medicine wheel, Celtic ceremonies, early Christian rituals and Balinese methods. For further insight into how to utilise space clearing in your life, I highly recommend Karen Kingston's book *Creating Sacred Space with Feng Shui* or Denise Linn's book *Sacred Space*.

Nine Star Ki Astrology

There are many different forms of Oriental Astrology and several are directly linked to the *I Ching*. Nine Star or Nine House Astrology incorporates symbolism from the *I Ching* in determining an individual's natal star while at the same time uses the lo shu magic square to determine which house your natal star occupies in any given year, month or day.

Originating in Tibet, this system predates the Chinese animal system of astrology by one thousand years. Nine Star Ki Astrology is primarily a Japanese interpretation of this system which has been refined and honed down over the centuries and remains popular in Japan today. ('Ki' is the Japanese word for chi.) It is relatively simple to understand and practise and it can give you enormous insights into 'who you are', 'where you are', and directionology.

'Who you are' relates to your individual horoscope, which can be calculated fairly simply. The value in knowing who you are can give you valuable insights into what kind of career or journey you could be taking in life, as well as your relationship with others around you.

'Where you are' is the understanding of which house you occupy in any given month, year and even day. Using this system, we migrate through these different houses in cycles of nine. These houses can be interpreted in a similar way to the symbolism of the different sectors represented in the pa kua. In other words, you could find yourself in a particular year, month or day occupying a house that, for you, represents Water. Naturally this would be a time of stillness, winter, hibernation – an ideal time to study, reflect and chart your future. Knowing which house you occupy at any given time can be of great value as you chart your future.

With the interpretation of directionology in Nine Star Ki

Astrology, it is relatively simple to determine which directions are best suited when you make major moves in any given month or year. Working with the currents of chi is far more likely to bring you greater rewards while at the same time makes the journey less hazardous or difficult. When planning a move, these auspicious directions can be used wisely to help you determine its timing. Although not linked directly with spatial feng shui, Nine Star Ki Astrology has evolved from the same stable. It is practical and relatively simple to use, and the modern expression of an aspect of feng shui that has the potential to benefit you regarding decisions and moves.

Electromagnetic Pollution

Some of the greatest hazards of modern high-tech living are the extraordinary levels of electromagnetic pollution that we are all likely to be exposed to. Electromagnetic fields (EMFs) occur on mild levels in the natural world, but current research suggests that, compared to our forebears, we are now being bombarded with the equivalent of 200,000,000 times the amount of EMFs. Sources of EMFs range from electricity pylons transmitting their effects over a distance of up to a quarter of a mile, down to the humble bedside electric clock which can project its EMF up to six feet away. Other typical sources of EMFs within the home can include: microwave ovens, electric cookers, washing machines, night storage heaters, hair dryers, electric clocks, stereo systems, televisions, computers, electric blankets, mobile telephones, electric razors and fluorescent lighting. Even jewellery can pick up EMFs and transfer them to you via meridians and acupuncture points on the fingers and ears.

A leading authority on electromagnetic stress and the

author of *Electropollution*, Roger Coghill has researched the subject in depth and has made available a relatively small and inexpensive diagnostic tool called a FieldMouse (details on page 140). The FieldMouse can help you check for safe EMF levels within your home, and it certainly gives you a new perspective on those seemingly quiet, defenceless domestic appliances we share our homes with.

One of the best solutions to reduce EMFs within the home is to have an electrician fit a gadget which automatically cuts off the electric current at the mains when you are not using any electrical appliances. Effectively this creates a far better environment in the bedrooms and would minimise your use of electric current to basic domestic appliances such as the television. In addition, I can recommend two devices that plug into an electric socket and help to neutralise or eliminate the effects of geopathic stress and electromagnetic pollution. They are Raditech (available from the Dulwich Health Society, see page 140); and Helios, 1 (available from Jan Cisek, see page 141).

Geopathic Stress

The earth naturally creates its own electromagnetic field and underground disturbances in this field can have potentially harmful effects. Sources of abnormal electromagnetic energy include underground water, underground streams and caverns, as well as geological phenomena such as the presence of minerals, especially coal and oil. Man-made interferences include sewers, tunnels and mains electricity.

Much scientific research has been conducted on this subject over the past 70 years and it is becoming increasingly clear that geopathic stress needs to be taken seriously by the home-owner. Consider what you spend on a survey to check that the structure of your new home is sound. In the same way, it is wise to seek the opinion of a professional dowser to locate any possible sources of geopathic stress and advise you on how to eliminate it. You can dowse for geopathic stress yourself (see *Are You Sleeping in a Safe Place?* by Rolph Gordon on page 136) or consider contacting the British Society of Dowsers who hold a register of reputable geopathic stress dowsers.

From a feng shui perspective, geopathic stress has been understood for centuries but expressed naturally in terms of chi and meridians. Knowledge of mysterious underground energies and the ability to dowse their precise location is as integral to the Chinese feng shui tradition as it is to other geomantic traditions of the world. Remember that the aim of feng shui initially is to seek healthy chi and to avoid unhealthy chi (sha chi).

Earth acupuncture is a powerful remedy designed to cure unhealthy chi and transform it into healthy chi. For more details contact Richard Creightmore (see page 143).

7

Advice from the Experts

In this book I have outlined the principles of feng shui and presented you with an overview of different styles and approaches. I have also given you a practical, step-by-step guide to surveying your home using common-sense practices. At the same time it must be appreciated that this is only the first 'layer' of feng shui. If you feel the task is too great, or would like the advice of an expert, or feel you could benefit from the added insights of years of experience, then you could consider hiring a professional feng shui consultant.

How to Find a Consultant

Word-of-mouth recommendation is frequently the best way to find any professional who might give you advice – the reputation of a good doctor, dentist, surveyor or accountant is always passed on from a satisfied client to their friends.

Failing this, we naturally seek out a professional body that represents them. Since feng shui is relatively new in the West, there is currently no professional body to represent all feng shui consultants. However in Great Britain the Feng Shui Society was established in 1994 as an independent group designed to support its membership with low-cost feng shui events and a newsletter, together with an active network of feng shui teachers and consultants based in Great Britain.

In 1997, the Society appealed to its professional members to consider forming a professional body that could initially set a Code of Ethics for feng shui practitioners and later develop educational standards that would be a minimum background and education for anyone setting up as a feng shui consultant.

The 40 members of the Register of Consultants of the Feng Shui Society all helped to draft, agree and sign a voluntary Code of Ethics in 1997. I highly recommend that you consider using the services of the society's consultants, who use the initials 'RCFSS' (Registered Consultant Feng Shui Society) after their names.

Feng Shui Society Voluntary Code of Ethics

1. Consultations should be guided by a high level of personal integrity and compassion, never causing a client to be exploited. Practitioners of feng shui should deliver a professional service, act legally (whether paid or unpaid) and uphold before the public the dignity and reputation of feng shui.

2. It is considered important that consultants have well-developed inter-personal skills in relating to clients, ensuring their safety and confidence both physically and psychologically.

3. The terms of the business contract by way of a consultant who offers feng shui must be made clear to the client before the commencement.

4. When advertising professional services, consultants

should ensure accuracy and avoid exaggeration, unwarranted statements or misleading publicity.

5. Consultants may use the title RCFSS. This may be used for publicity, letter headings and business stationery.

6. It is expected consultants should conduct themselves in their feng shui related activities in ways which do not undermine public confidence in either their role as a consultant or in the work of other consultants.

7. It is understood that consultants are fully paid-up annual members of both the Register and the Society. Membership of the Register incorporates public liability insurance.

8. Individuals wishing to be Registered consultants of the Feng Shui Society are expected to show evidence to support fifty consultations and to maintain ongoing professional development.

9. All consultants who are registered with the Feng Shui Society have signed and agreed to abide by this voluntary Code of Ethics. While the Society is happy to deal with complaints about individual consultants who are registered with them, they cannot speak for or represent consultants who are not members of the Register.

For further details about the Society, see p. 138

What to Expect from a Consultation

The following guidelines were all agreed by members of the Register of Consultants of the Feng Shui Society. It is vital to agree a fee in advance and to be absolutely sure what this will cover. Apart from the consultation itself, does this take into account any follow-up telephone conversations, include a written report and cover any travel expenses? Try to establish a fee for the job rather than an hourly rate which could cause the possibility of dispute at the end. It is my strong advice to avoid anyone who asks for payment for special blessings or esoteric cures to be conducted after the consultation for an additional fee.

Even if you have arranged a flat-rate fee for the job in advance, do ask roughly how long the consultation is going to take. As a basic guideline, an average-sized family home could take between one and a half to three hours. It is important to remember that many consultants do a lot of work in advance, making calculations about your property and your relationship with it based on your date of birth and the compass direction of your front door.

Many different schools and styles of feng shui are now available. To avoid dispute, confusion and misunderstanding, be very clear in advance what style of feng shui the practitioner uses. Naturally, if you have done some reading on the subject, you are going to have certain expectations as to what they may do or advise in the consultation, and if you know where they are coming from in advance, then it only makes the consultation more interesting and more educational. Many feng shui practitioners have additional skills which you can find out about when you ask for the current list of Registered Practitioners from the Feng Shui Society. In addition to feng shui, you may feel you need extra help from an expert in dowsing for geopathic stress, space clearing or earth acupuncture, or you may want to consult an architect or an interior designer for advice to go alongside the feng shui recommendations.

Be clear in advance what kind of reasonable follow-up contact you can expect from after their visit. From your angle and from theirs, it is only fair to establish what is reasonable in terms of follow-up at no further cost to yourself.

Finally, it is very important that you are clear what you want from the consultation, that your expectations are reasonable and that you are also willing to be responsible for following through on the advice given. The more focused you are about what you would like to achieve and the more involved you (and other household occupants) become, then the more likely it is you will achieve successful results. Regard a feng shui consultation as a real partnership between you and the consultant. They have, after all, many years of experience but your will, your intention and your accuracy in following their advice is just as important.

8

Taking it Further

Practice

Feng shui is undoubtedly a profound and fascinating subject. I would suggest that initially you practise the ideas only within your own home, having first made sure that the environment is clean and clutter-free! Avoid the mistake of making hundreds of small adjustments and cures — implement a few basic changes, if they are needed, and start to notice the difference. Some changes are quite dramatic and can happen almost instantly, while others are more subtle and can take up to a month to manifest. It really is not wise to offer your unsolicited feng shui advice to your friends and neighbours — lend them a book instead.

One of the greatest learning tools that we can rely on is the simple act of observation. Just looking around, you are surrounded by a fascinating environment with all kinds of examples of poor or great feng shui. Wear your feng shui 'glasses' next time you are out on a walk. Look out for evidence of sha chi in the layout of roads, car parks or a local housing estate. Wander round a church, a museum, or a railway station, a successful restaurant, an art gallery or a shopping mall. They may not necessarily have been designed around feng shui principles but notice where almost intuitively they either benefit from it or have created a feng shui nightmare for themselves. A little knowledge has always been dangerous, so keep up your practice by watching and observing.

Reading

Already from this book you may have a sense of the kind of feng shui you would like to know more about. On pages 135–7 I have given you a list of many useful books. If you do not want to buy them yourself, simply ask your library and they will order them for you. Remember that the books may offer what appears to be conflicting advice. However, the fundamental principles are the same. Only the practice is being expressed and utilised in different ways. There are no rights, and no wrongs!

In 1998, a new monthly glossy magazine called *Feng Shui for Modern Living* was launched to bring a greater awareness of feng shui to the public. It is available on most news-stands.

Study

Plenty of courses are currently on offer in Great Britain. Some teachers and consultants offer introductory weekend courses and a growing number of professionals are setting up professional training in feng shui. There is great value in signing up for a weekend workshop in feng shui as it helps bring the subject alive and introduces you to other people who are at the same point of learning. Without any major financial outlay you can test the water to see if this is something you would wish to pursue further. You are always going to learn something, especially if you attend with an open mind and a blank notebook.

As far as professional training is concerned, I would highly recommend that you get the prospectus from the school, attend an open evening, request to meet the director or some of the teachers and, best of all, get an inspiring recommendation from one of their graduates. With no fully integrated or agreed standards currently in place within the different schools offering feng shui, it is really up to you to use your best judgement. The hours that you may spend in the classroom are not as important as the skill of the teachers and the encouragement the school provides for you to personally practise the system and be supported in your development as a feng shui consultant.

In traditional times feng shui was regarded as a lifetime study and practice, so it cannot be compared to an intensive six-week computer course. Information has to be learned and assimilated, but it also needs to mature and develop. We live in a culture that is driven by measurable results. At school and university we complete courses and take examinations and either pass or fail, all within a finite timeframe. What intrigued me when I studied martial arts was that I signed up to a course that seemed endless. I asked the master how many weeks it would take for me to get my yellow belt. His answer was, 'Wait.' When I asked 'Well, *roughly* how long is this going to take?' His answer was, 'When I say you are ready.' Feng shui is much the same. There is theory, and there is practice, but ultimately you need to combine the two, with feng shui becoming an integral part of your life as you appreciate shape, form and chi in your surroundings.

Almost every Chinese feng shui expert I have met has benefited from their own chi development. Any practice you can incorporate into your life to give you greater under-standing of chi and all of its manifestations will make it easier for you to develop your skills with feng shui. Many practi-tioners that I know use chi kung, tai chi, a martial art or some form of spiritual practice to enhance their awareness. Some eat simply and live frugally, while others are ostentatious and lively. Deep down, they all have one thing in common, and that is a profound appreciation and harnessing of vital chi energy in their own lives.

I sincerely hope you take this fascinating subject further, and that it brings new insights into your life and relation-ships, not only with space, but also with other people. I wish you and your family abundant health and prosperity and I would appreciate any useful comments or feedback (see page 143)

Good luck!

Glossary

Bagua: CPO *pa kua*.
cardinal points: North, South, East, West.
chi: 'cosmic breath'.
Compass School: school of feng shui which utilises the lo p'an compass to assess chi movement.
Earlier Heaven arrangement: arrangement of the eight trigrams in a circular formation, primarily for protection.
feng: wind.
feng sha: poisonous wind.
feng shui hsien-sheng: a feng shui master.
Five Elements: Water, Fire, Earth, Metal, Wood.
Form School: use of the landscape to assess auspicious chi flow.
hexagram: a formation of eight broken or unbroken lines formed from two trigrams. There are sixty-four different hexagrams.
I Ching: *The Book of Changes*, a Chinese classic based on the sixty-four hexagrams.
intercardinal points: South-west, South-east, North-west, North-east.

kua: see *trigram*.

Later Heaven arrangement: an arrangement of the eight trigrams in a circular formation. Used extensively in feng shui calculations.

lo p'an/luo pan: the feng shui compass.

lo shu: Taoist magic square with nine houses associated with the Later Heaven arrangement of trigrams.

lung: dragon.

lung mei: dragon meridians or veins.

lung shen: dragon spirits.

magic square: see *lo shu*.

pa kua: (also known as bagua) an eight-sided or circular arrangement of the eight trigrams.

'poison arrow': see *secret arrow*.

'secret arrow': (also known as poison arrow) a potentially destructive influence of negative chi from nearby roofs or properties.

sha chi: stagnant chi.

shen: spirits.

shui: water.

shui-lung: water dragon.

Taoism: Chinese belief in the Tao — 'the way' — concerned with harmony and flow.

trigram: *(also known as kua)* three horizontal lines, broken or unbroken, respectively representing yin or yang. There are eight in total. Two trigrams form the basis of a hexagram.

yang: active or activating energy.

yin: passive or sedentary energy.

Further Reading

Feng Shui

Simon Brown, *Principles of Feng Shui*, Thorsons, 1996

Lam Kam Chuen, *The Feng Shui Handbook*, Gaia Books, 1995

Dennis Fairchild, *Healing Homes, Feng Shui: Here and Now*, Wavefield Books, 1996

Man-Ho Kwok, *The Elements of Feng Shui*, Element Books, 1991

Man-Ho Kwok, *The Feng Shui Kit*, Piatkus, 1995

Gina Lazenby, *Feng Shui House Book*, Conran Octopus, 1998

Evelyn Lip, *Chinese Geomancy*, Times Books International, Singapore, 1979

Raymond Lo, *Feng Shui: The Pillars of Destiny*, Times Books International, Singapore, 1994

Sarah Rossbach, *Feng Shui*, Rider, 1984

Sarah Rossbach, *Interior Design with Feng Shui*, Rider, 1987

Raphael Simons, *Feng Shui Step by Step*, Rider, 1996

Stephen Skinner, *Feng Shui*, Parragon, 1997

Stephen Skinner, *The Living Earth Manual of Feng Shui*, Routledge & Kegan Paul, 1982

William Spear, *Feng Shui Made Easy*, Thorsons, 1995

Lillian Too, *The Complete Illustrated Guide to Feng Shui*, Element Books, 1996

Derek Walters, *Feng Shui Handbook*, Aquarian Press, 1991

Richard Webster, *Feng Shui for Beginners*, Llewellyn Publications, 1997

Eva Wong, *Feng Shui: The Ancient Wisdom of Harmonious Living for Modern Times*, Shambhala, 1996

Space Clearing

Karen Kingston, *Creating Sacred Space with Feng Shui*, Piaktus, 1996

Denise Linn, *Sacred Space*, Rider, 1995

Clearing Clutter

Declan Treacy, *Clear Your Desk*, Century Business, 1992

Feng Shui Gardening

Gill Hale, *The Feng Shui Garden*, Asiapac Books, 1998

Electromagnetic Stress

Roger Coghill, *Electro Pollution,* Thorsons, 1990

Dr Glen Startwout, *Electromagnetic Pollution Solutions*, Aerai Publishing, Hawaii, 1991

Dowsing

Sig Lonegren, *Sig Lonegren's Dowsing Rod Kit*, Virgin Books, 1995

Geopathic Stress

Rolf Gordon, *Are You Sleeping in a Safe Place?*, The Dulwich Health Society, 130 Gypsy Hill, London SE19 1PL

Jane Thurnell-Read, *Geopathic Stress*, Element,1995

Nine Star Ki Astrology

Bob Sachs, *The Complete Guide to Nine Star Ki*, Element, 1994
Jon Sandifer, *Feng Shui Astrology*, Piatkus, 1997
Takashi Yoshikawa, *The Ki*, Rider, 1998

Useful Addresses

The Feng Shui Society

The Feng Shui Society was established in 1993 as an unincor-
porated, non-profitmaking association formed to advance
feng shui principles and concepts as a contribution to the
creation of harmonious environments for individuals and
society in general. The Society serves as a focus for the
exchange of information and experience, both of the professional feng shui community and for others wishing to develop
their knowledge and apply the principles in their own lives.
The feng shui Society offers members:

☆ A programme of Society events throughout the country

☆ Discussion groups and case studies

☆ A bimonthly newsletter with articles and book reviews

☆ A book, video and tape library

☆ Access to the registered consultants list

For further details please contact:
The Feng Shui Society
377 Edgware Road
London
W2 1BT
tel: 07050 289200
website: http://www.netcomuk.co.uk/kayers/fengshui/html

International Contacts

Feng Shui Society of Australia
PO Box 6416
Shopping World
NSW 2060
Australia

Feng Shui Guild
PO Box 766
Boulder
CO 80306–0766
USA

Feng Shui Warehouse
PO Box 6689
San Diego
CA 92166
USA

Feng Shui France
40 Avenue Guy de Maupassant
78400 Chatou
France

Further Resources

Feng Shui Books, Windchimes, Crystals

FSNI Mail Order
PO Box 9
Pateley Bridge
Harrogate HG3 5XG

The Geomancer
PO Box 250
Woking
Surrey GU21 1YY

The Feng Shui Company
37 Ballard House
Norway Street
London SE10 9DD

Esoterica
5a Devonshire Road
London W4 2EU

Electromagnetic Stress Detectors and Eliminators

Coghill Research Laboratories
Lower Race
Pontypool
Gwent NP4 5UF

Geopathic Stress Eliminators

Dulwich Health Society
130 Gypsy Hill
London SE19 1PL

Jan Cisek
8 The Warwick
68 Richmond Hill
Richmond
Surrey TW10 6RH

Space Clearing

Karen Kingston Promotions
tel: 07000 772232
email: UKoffice@spaceclearing.com

Feng Shui Websites

Feng Shui Emporium
http://www.luckycat.com

Feng Shui Society
http://www.fengshuisociety.org.uk

Lillian Too
http://www.asiaconnect.com.my/lillian-too

Denise Linn
http://denise@qed-productions.com

Feng Shui Interior Design
http://www.pdc.net./idd/FengShui.htm

Feng Shui for Modern Living
http://www.fengshui—magazine.com

William Spear
http://members.aol.com/fengshuime/wmhtml

Feng Shui Courses

Organisations and individuals who currently offer training
and/or certification:

Feng Shui Network International
PO Box 2133
London W1A 1RL

The Imperial School of Feng Shui
34 Banbury Road
Ettington
Stratford-upon-Avon
Warwickshire CV37 7SU

Feng Shui Worldwide
55a Winchester Road
Four Marks
Alton
Hants GU34 5HG

The Feng Shui Company
37 Ballard House
Norway Street
London SE10 9DD

Richard Creightmore
Landscope
Beech View
Crowborough Road
Nutley
East Sussex
TN22 3HY

Jon Sandifer (see below)

Workshops and Consultations with Jon Sandifer

For details of my consultation service in the London area or for information on my courses in London or my teaching schedule worldwide, please contact me at:

Jon Sandifer
PO Box 69
Teddington
Middlesex TW11 9SH
fax: 0181 977 8988
email: Jon-Sandifer@compuserve.com
website: http://www.sandifer.demon.co.uk

Index

Page numbers in *italic* refer to the illustrations

Piatkus Guides, written by experts, combine background information with practical exercises, and are designed to change the way you live. Titles include:

Tarot   Cassandra Eason

Tarot's carefully graded advice enables readers to obtain excellent readings from Day One. You will quickly gain a thorough knowledge of both Major and Minor Arcanas and their symbolism, and learn how to use a variety of Tarot spreads.

Meditation   Bill Anderton

Meditation covers the origins, theory and benefits of meditation. It includes over 30 meditations and provides all the advice you need to meditate successfully.

Crystal Wisdom   Andy Baggott & Sally Morningstar

Crystal Wisdom is a fascinating guide to the healing power of crystals. It details the history and most popular modern uses of crystals and vibrational healing. It also covers colour, sound and chakra healing, and gem, crystal and flower essences.

Celtic Wisdom   Andy Baggott

Celtic Wisdom is a dynamic introduction to this popular subject. The author covers Celtic spirituality, the wisdom of trees, animals and stones, ritual and ceremony and much more.

Feng Shui   Jon Sandifer

Feng Shui introduces the origins, theory and practice of the Chinese art of perfect placement, or geomancy. It provides easy-to-follow techniques to help you carry out your own readings and create an auspicious living space.

Essential Nostradamus   Peter Lemesurier

...tial Nostradamus charts the life of this extraordinary
*...*cludes newly discovered facts about his life and
*...*surier unravels his prophecies for the coming
decades.